MW00417126

Endless
and
Proper
Work

Our Endless and Proper Work

Starting (and Sticking to) Your Writing Practice

Ron Hogan

Belt Publishing

Copyright © 2021 by Ron Hogan
Illustrations © 2021 by Emm Roy

All rights reserved. This book or any portion thereof may not be
reproduced or used in any manner whatsoever without the express
written permission of the publisher except for the use of brief
quotations in a book review.

Printed in the United States of America
First edition 2021
1 2 3 4 5 6 7 8 9

ISBN: 978-1-948742-94-8

Belt Publishing
5322 Fleet Avenue
Cleveland, Ohio 44105
www.beltpublishing.com

Cover art by David Wilson
Illustrations by Emm Roy
Book design by Meredith Pangrace

Thanks, Laura!

TABLE OF CONTENTS

Introduction p.9

Chapter One: What We Carry in Our Hearts p.13

Chapter Two: An Adventure into an Unknown World p.25

Chapter Three: Our Endless and Proper Work......................... p.37

Chapter Four: Reclaiming Your Time for Writing p.49

Chapter Five: Finding Your Groove p.61

Chapter Six: Your Voice Is Valuable p.77

Chapter Seven: Pacing Yourself for the Long Haul p.97

Chapter Eight: Destroy Your Safe and Happy Lives p.105

Acknowledgments..p.121

Resources (An Incomplete Reckoning)...................................p.122

Introduction

This book emerged out of a newsletter I launched in 2018 called "Destroy Your Safe and Happy Lives," an allusion to the opening line of a Mekons song that sounded a lot more exuberantly rebellious before the COVID-19 pandemic knocked the entire planet off-balance.

I earn a living partly through editorial consulting, which is pretty much exactly what it sounds like: I'll read a client's manuscript, then offer feedback on what's working and what isn't so they have some ideas about how to approach their next draft. As they're reviewing my notes and deciding whether or not they want to move forward, they'll often ask: "Would it be worth it? Do you think this is publishable?"

The end goal for aspiring writers *always* seemed to be "getting a book deal" or "getting published," and the more I thought about it, the more I realized I wasn't entirely happy about that. The newsletter was a way for me to address that issue.

Don't get me wrong: Being a professional writer is one of the best jobs around, even though it can be one of the hardest. It's certainly one of the most fulfilling jobs I've ever had, emotionally if not always financially. If you can do it well, and do well at it, you absolutely should.

But the real value of writing isn't in the money you can make. We accept a certain recreational value for all sorts of creative endeavors without any thought of generating a new revenue stream for ourselves. Plenty of people want to learn an instrument without eying a career as a professional musician, or take up drawing or painting without expecting to end up with a gallery showcase. Start writing, though, and, before too long, if you're not asking yourself whether you're going to try to get published, the people around you who know you're writing probably will.

Why, though? Why is it considered normal to develop a technical proficiency at, say, painting watercolors just for the fun of expressing yourself creatively, while writing is expected to "earn its keep," so to speak? What if we thought about writing as a personal process of self-discovery, a way of gravitating toward stories and themes you feel passionately about and learning more about those passions as you go along—and learning how to share that passion with others?

Again, I'm not judging anybody for wanting to make money by being a writer, not least of all because that's a path I've chosen at various points in my life. You'll notice, for example, that I'm not giving this book away. If you're *just* looking to make money, though, there are so many easier ways to do it. And while I concede the possibility that you can write a commercially viable book, maybe even more than one, without going through the process of self-discovery, I have to tell you it doesn't seem like it would be personally fulfilling.

(No, really, I *have* to tell you that, and believe it. Otherwise I'm gonna go into an existential tailspin.)

Ultimately, I suppose, "Is this ever going to be publishable?" is not all that different a question from "Can I share this with readers?" It's just a matter of emphasis, after all. But when you're just starting out, when you don't have any contractual commitments, when it's just you and the empty screen or the blank sheet of paper, it's the second question that will lead you to better writing . . . and make it easier, if you ultimately decide to seek publication, for your book to wind up in someone else's hands.

That's what this book is about.

WHAT IF WE THOUGHT ABOUT
WRITING AS A PERSONAL PROCESS
OF SELF-DISCOVERY, A WAY OF
GRAVITATING TOWARDS STORIES
AND THEMES YOU FEEL PASSIONATELY
ABOUT AND LEARNING MORE ABOUT
THOSE PASSIONS AS YOU GO
ALONG—AND LEARNING HOW TO
SHARE THAT PASSION WITH OTHERS?

Chapter One:

What We Carry in Our Hearts

I n February 2020, the Authors Guild issued a report called "The Profession of Author in the 21st Century." At its heart, the report was a stark warning that "the career of full-time professional author has become endangered," and the economic reality it outlined to drive that point home was staggering: The median book-related income for a full-time writer in 2017 was just $20,300, and most writers weren't even doing that well. In fact, 54 percent of those surveyed reported the income their books generated that year was less than the federal poverty benchmark of $12,488.

Some writers fared better, of course. The top 10 percent of the survey respondents reported a median book-related income of $167,000. (Remember, a median isn't an *average*, it's a midpoint—so the actual incomes those high-performing writers claimed for themselves ranged from $84,200 all the way up to $9,300,000.) At the opposite end of the spectrum, 20 percent of the writers polled said they hadn't made *any income at all* from their books that year.

The Authors Guild exists to advocate for the economic viability of the writing profession, and their report does an excellent job of reviewing the trends in the publishing and bookselling industries that have created this situation. Cultural trends, too: They note that people are reading—and, more to the point, *buying*—fewer books than they used to, and, thanks to Amazon, expecting the books they do buy, especially the ebooks, to be cheaper than ever. That means less money for publishing houses, which leads to less money making its way to every writer's bank account.

As the best-selling thriller writer Douglas Preston puts it, many aspiring writers may fall prey to what he calls "censorship of the marketplace," abandoning their potential writing careers before they've even really begun. They simply won't be able to afford to do it full-time, and there's little incentive to pursue a side hustle writing around your day job and all your other responsibilities and obligations when there are so many other, more relaxing ways to spend those few spare moments.

Long story short, if, as Samuel Johnson said, no man but a blockhead ever wrote, except for money, just about nobody but a blockhead would go into writing thinking they were going to be the rare person who makes a living wage from it.

But you know what? That's fine.

If you want to be a writer because you want to make a lot of money, let me give you some advice: Don't. Go to business school, go to medical school—heck, go to law school. Or learn a trade. You'll probably do a lot better for yourself on any of those paths than you would as a full-time writer. You might even make enough money that you could dedicate some spare time to writing on the side.

If you want to become a writer so you can become famous, my advice to you is also: Don't. As a rule, book people don't get famous, although sometimes famous people get book deals. (As for the books that come out of those deals, well, it's always a pleasant surprise when one of them turns out to be genuinely interesting.) Think about it: How many authors do you know that are actually celebrities? I don't mean that you know who they are because they're your favorite authors, I mean *celebrities*—the kind of people who could be recognized by complete strangers on a city street hundreds of miles away from their hometown. Stephen King used to be that famous, and maybe he still is. James Patterson might be, I think, thanks to all those TV commercials he's made for his novels. J. K. Rowling? Possibly. Beyond those three, though, I'm drawing a blank.

What if you didn't look at writing as a stepping-stone to fame and fortune, though?

Obviously, everybody likes to be compensated for their efforts. Everybody likes to be recognized for what they've accomplished. But I believe we write, first and foremost, because we have something we want to share with the world.

We write to *inform*—to share the knowledge we've acquired through research or experience, to express our opinions, to call attention to something we think more people ought to be noticing.

We also write to *entertain*—to give people a cathartic emotional experience (usually, but not always, a happy one), or to get them excited about something that excites us, to feel passion for something we feel passionate about.

Often, you'll want to inform *and* entertain—to inspire people to take action, for example, or encourage them to feel empathy for real or fictional people (or other living creatures).

We write because we feel *compelled* to share these things with others. People sometimes talk about writing as an almost therapeutic experience, and sometimes there's an element of truth to that. We may be writing to process or make sense of something we've experienced, or something we've learned.

That's not all there is to it, though. We're almost never just writing for ourselves. If we were just going through that whole process for ourselves, why would we be putting everything down on paper (or on a hard drive) instead of just thinking our way through it? Okay, sometimes it's useful to have a written record so you can better organize your thoughts and refresh your memory. That's true. Even then, though, I'd argue that there's an implicit audience in the very act of writing, that—consciously or unconsciously—we want to share what we've written with someone else, even if we don't know who it is as we're writing.

And when you feel that desire to share the things you're most passionate about strongly enough, the economic hurdles won't hold you back. You might not know how you'll ever be able to make money from it, let alone enough money to be able to dedicate yourself to doing nothing else. But that's not going to stop you from pouring your heart out on the page (or the keyboard) and then fine-tuning the results over and over.

———————

In an ideal world, we'd know before we started writing what that thing we're compelled to write is, and for some people it actually does work that way. The rest of us, though, have to start with a fuzzy notion of a "theme" (or "mission," or "vision") that only becomes recognizable as we take the time to write around it. We have to keep making a conscious decision to work toward better understanding that theme, so we'll be able to express it as clearly as possible to the rest of the world.

Achieving that clarity is the goal of every decision we make about writing, from finding the time to do it to revising the manuscript *yet again*. And all those decisions, all those efforts, are worth it, because they make us better writers.

There's a quote from the twentieth-century Trappist monk Thomas Merton that sums this up perfectly, I think:

> Life consists in learning to live on one's own, spontaneous, freewheeling: to do this one must recognize what is one's own—be familiar and at home with oneself. This means basically learning who one is, and learning what one has to offer to the contemporary world, and then learning how to make that offering valid.

Instead of looking at writing as a way to find a story, what if we see it as a way of learning who *we* are, of better understanding *ourselves* in order to then be able to communicate with everyone else at a meaningful level?

To do that, we need to have a certain amount of self-comfort—which is not the same thing as being free from anxiety. I don't think any of us is ever completely free from worrying that we're getting something wrong on the page, whether it's that we're not being clear enough or that we're being pathetically blatant and obvious. We can, however, become comfortable enough to recognize that anxiety for what it is, and to look as objectively as possible at what's on the page—and, ideally, have someone we trust speak honestly with us about it—then fix what's wrong and trust in what's right.

In the larger project of living one's life that Merton had in mind, meditation and contemplative prayer played a major role in developing one's self-awareness, and he believed not only that the mind "finds best when it stops seeking," but that "the graduate level of learning is when one learns to sit still and be what one has become."

Here, too, we can draw a parallel to a writing practice; in fact, it's not any kind of stretch to see writing as a form of contemplation. Sometimes, when we start out, we find ourselves "writing to the theme," then becoming frustrated when what's on the page doesn't seem to fit what we want to say. But we're not sure how to fix it, because we're still not really sure what we want to say.

The more time you spend getting the raw ideas out of your head and examining them in their incomplete state, the easier it may become to recognize the fundamental concepts behind what you're writing. You may find that what you really wanted to say begins to emerge more clearly—not because you've beat yourself over the head, torturing yourself until you get it right, but simply because you've kept at it. Deeply considering the thoughts you've consciously shaped and the ones that emerge unbidden, testing them all, then building upon the ones that ring true. Over and over again, repeating as often as necessary.

I have a longstanding daily devotional reading practice, and one of the books I've read through that practice is *You Are the Beloved*, a sort of "greatest hits" compilation of quotations from the late Catholic theologian Henri Nouwen, who I've sometimes described to people as a cross between Thomas Merton and Mister Rogers.

This is one of the passages I came across in my reading:

> Writing is a process in which we discover what lives in us. The writing itself reveals to us what is alive in us. . . . To write is to embark on a journey whose final destination we do not know. Thus, writing requires a real act of trust. We have to say to ourselves: "I do not

yet know what I carry in my heart, but I trust that it will emerge as I write."

Reading those lines reinforced my growing belief that the writing life is about recognizing what it is that you need to share with the world, then making yourself into the person who is capable of that act of sharing. And I'm not just talking about craft, about developing the skills to tell your story clearly in a compelling voice. That's a big part of it, but there's another fundamental aspect we probably don't talk about as much as we should—the process of becoming someone who has the inner clarity to recognize their story and the confidence to open themselves up to others in the sharing of it.

(When I say "story," by the way, you can also read that as "message," if you're coming from a particular nonfictional mindset. Or "poem," if that's your thing.)

I believe Nouwen is right; many of us do start out with a nebulous idea of "what we carry in our hearts," and even if we start out with a firm grasp on our intentions, we can get into the middle of the writing and realize that while we've been *close*, the story we're actually here to share has been just beyond us.

Once we've found it, though, will we be ready to embrace it? Will we be ready to do the mental and emotional work (not to mention the physical labor of writing) that will go into telling this story the way it needs to be told? Will we be ready to acknowledge that people will not only judge this story, but they may also (especially if we're talking about certain nonfiction genres, like memoir) judge us for telling this story? How some stranger judges us for telling our stories isn't relevant, of course, but we don't always remember that, and, as a result, we let their judgments affect us.

Are we prepared to change course, if that's what the story requires of us? That's a question I grapple with a lot, especially in my newspaper writing. I may start out with one idea of how I want to write about a topic, only to realize as I'm doing the research, or maybe not until my editor hands back her notes on my first draft, that a better approach to the material exists. *These* things I thought were so important turn out to be less significant than *those* things, and I have to decide: Am I ready to let go of the story I've been carrying around in my head, and to push myself to tell this new story?

Wait, you might be thinking. What makes my editor's idea about the story "more right" than my own? What if your original concept really is the one that speaks to your heart, and you don't *want* to tell another version that feels phony to you? That's a legitimate position, and ultimately you'll only know the right course to take when you're actually facing that situation. I've been fortunate enough to work with editors who have a strong sense of story, and who regularly challenge me to do my best work. When they ask me to try something new, it's almost always something that forces me to dig deeper into myself, to shake off my assumptions so I can see things in the story I wasn't able to see before.

That takes me back to Nouwen's description of writing as a process of discovery—but also a process of *transformation* as well as creation. As he puts it elsewhere in the same passage, "Writing is like giving away the few loaves and fishes one has, trusting that they will multiply in the giving." You start to write, and then you sit there, staring at the notepad or the journal or the computer screen, trying to figure out what to do with what you've got. Then you get an idea, and you lay it down, and you start staring again, and you get another idea, and you keep on going, creating something from what you thought was—well, not "nothing," I suppose, but maybe "barely anything."

Or you set down a whole lot of material, more than you could ever possibly use, things that don't even fit together, and then you look at it all and find the bits that do work, and you pull them out, and then you figure out what's missing so you can tie those bits together . . .

However you get it done, from a strictly material standpoint, it would be wrong to say, "The story was there all along, you just had to come and find it." A more accurate way to put it might be, "The *potential* to tell a story was there all along, you just had to come and cultivate it."

More and more, I've come to understand the writing life as a process of recognizing and cultivating that potential.

———

By now, you've probably noticed how frequently I draw upon spiritual metaphors to describe the writing practice and its results. I try not to lean particularly far into that language, because my spirituality might not be your spirituality, and you likely didn't come here for spiritual advice. (And, too, because I'm still sorting out what my spirituality is, exactly.)

Sometimes, though, the perfect metaphor for the writing life comes from a spiritual corner, and that's why I'm going to tell you about Saint Lutgardis, the medieval mystic whose feast day also happens to be my birthday, which is how I came to know of her.

Lutgardis was an early thirteenth-century nun who had several mystical visions of Jesus, including one in which he offered her a gift. She wanted to learn Latin: "I wish that I might understand the Psalter through which I pray so that I might be more devout." So Jesus bestowed that knowledge upon her, but after a few days, she came to him and asked if she could trade it back. For what, Jesus asked? "I want your heart," she told him.

In her vision, Jesus said, no, I want *your* heart, and reached into her and took out her heart and replaced it with his own. (All of this is from the life of Lutgardis written by Thomas of Cantimpré, who got the story directly from her.)

This is, essentially, a foundation for the mystical tradition of the Sacred Heart, the representation of Christ's compassion for humanity. And though, as I said before, I'm not evangelizing here, I do think there's something in this story you can apply to your writing practice.

It is, of course, a simple and obvious interpretation: Knowledge is great, but it can only get you so far. If you want to *understand* something (or someone), you need to be able to approach it (or them) with compassion and empathy. You need to be able to open your heart and allow the encounter to transform you.

A successful writing practice doesn't automatically reaffirm what you already know. It might end up doing that, but only after you've been through the process of looking at that thing you think you understand from every possible angle, from living with it and contemplating it and really *seeing* it for the first time. And "that thing" can be a story you've made up, it can be an event that's taken place out in the world, it can be your innermost self . . .

A successful writing practice prepares you for those moments of revelation, fosters an environment in which they can take place. I'm not saying you're going to get struck by a series of mystical visions. I'm saying that you're creating a space in your life where insight is attainable, but more importantly, where you can become the person who is capable of recognizing those insights, then acting upon them.

IF YOU KNOW WHAT YOU'RE HERE TO DO, AND YOU'RE DOING IT, YOU DON'T HAVE TO WORRY WHEN SOMEBODY DOESN'T GET IT. YOU JUST HAVE TO BELIEVE THAT SOMEONE ELSE WILL.

Chapter Two:

An Adventure into an
Unknown World

The last time my wife, Laura, and I went to Los Angeles, I took her to the Museum of Jurassic Technology. It was her first time there and my first visit in more than twenty years. I was surprised by how little it had changed; the main gallery on the first floor seemed exactly as I had remembered it from the mid-1990s, and it felt as if the new exhibits had been integrated seamlessly into the layout.

It can be hard to describe the museum to someone who's never heard of it. I'd tried to explain to my wife's relatives where we were going earlier that day, and I eventually settled on telling them, "It's like a museum-sized performance art installation." Or you could describe it as an Andy Kaufman-esque blurring of the lines between museum and artwork. Some of the exhibits are real, while a few are elaborately constructed . . . well, *hoaxes* seems a terribly judgmental word, and *fables* implies a didacticism that isn't really part of the museum's atmosphere. Let's go with *stories*—narratives where the weird and the mundane nestle comfortably together.

There's one tiny alcove where you sit through a slideshow recounting the life of Hagop Sandaldjian in painstaking detail, all as a prelude to the presentation of three "microminiature" sculptures that Sandaldjian fit within (or, in the case of Goofy, atop) the eye of a needle. It's not a short presentation—I didn't check the time, but let's say somewhere between five and ten minutes—and in some ways, like many of the museum's multimedia exhibits, it veers into the parodically boring.

After it was through, we continued to wander through the rooms and finally Laura asked me, "So how much of this is real?" Because she had been totally prepared to accept that the Hagop Sandaldjian exhibit was an elaborate joke—until she pulled up his Wikipedia page.

I remembered that moment a few days later, on the plane back to New York, as I was reading the book I'd bought in the museum's gift shop, Lawrence Weschler's *Mr. Wilson's Cabinet of Wonder.* I'd read it back in the '90s, and it turned me into a lifelong Weschler fan, but I'd forgotten many of the specific details of his own efforts to verify some of the exhibits—and to understand the museum's founder and curator, David Wilson.

The reason reading that book took me back to Laura's question is that here I was, engrossed once again in Weschler's expeditions through university research libraries, trying to track down any stray clues to the mysteries onto which he stumbled, while she had just taken her iPhone out of her bag and found answers within seconds. It occurred to me that the Museum of Jurassic Technology was a much different experience in the pre-Wikipedia era, in that you truly had to surrender yourself to David Wilson's vision. Even after you left the building, probing the museum's mysteries would take significant effort—and the results might well prove inconclusive.

There's a sign in the lobby of the museum banning cell phone use of any kind. I saw it during our visit and I figured, *Okay, yes, this is a carefully crafted environment. It doesn't need to be disrupted by people yapping on their phones or taking flash photos.* Now, though, I see that it was also a way to (at least try to) keep people from looking stuff up as they wandered through the rooms, because that would only break the spell.

One of the big lessons of the Museum of Jurassic Technology is that the world is a weird and wonderful place, and that if we approach it with a mixture of awe and skeptical inquiry, it can yield up marvelous treasures. There's a straightforward lesson to be drawn from this about how writers should approach the world, but I also want to touch upon what David Wilson's museum can teach us how we present our work to readers— which is to say, I want to suggest that immersing readers in an overwhelming experience, whether it's fiction or nonfiction, is . . . well, maybe it's not *the* thing we should be striving for, but it's certainly *a* thing to strive for.

That's a tall order, of course, and you can't expect everything you write to do that for everybody who reads it. Maybe it's enough, though, to create something some people will be able to enjoy on a straightforward level, while a handful of readers will experience something more profound, more inspiring, through their encounter with your work. It doesn't have to be an overt message. It can even be a weird, unsettling story they aren't quite sure they believe, and yet they can't fully shake . . . like a strange museum dropped in the middle of an otherwise ordinary neighborhood.

While we're on the subject of literature and overwhelming experiences, Laura and I have an annual tradition, every December, of watching the Alastair Sim version of *A Christmas Carol.* One year, I found myself considering how much

Charles Dickens's story has shaped our modern understanding of Christmas and the way we celebrate the holiday. I think that all of us, at some level, like to imagine that something we write will change the world. Dickens actually did it!

That is a compelling metric for "literary" success . . . against which many of us would undoubtedly fall short. It's like dreaming about being a bestselling author: You might be able to pull it off, with the right combination of talent and circumstance, but most of us won't. Even so, we shouldn't regard ourselves as failures.

One way to look at this is to avoid focusing on *how many* lives our writing might change, and just embrace the possibility of changing *any lives at all.* Think of the books that have changed your life—the ones that have opened your mind to new possibilities, that brought your questions and concerns into a new focus, that set you off on a new path. I imagine some of those books are "classics" or "Great Books," but I'm willing to bet at least one of them isn't. It might be the kind of book that, when you recommend it to others, they might tell you they've never heard of it, or maybe they've heard of it but never come across it, or they never felt an urgent need to read it, not with so many other books out there . . .

Although the author of that book might not have enjoyed wealth or fame as a result of writing it, they still managed to make a difference in your life. And it's entirely possible you could be that writer for somebody else if you stick to your writing practice.

The first book I can remember doing that for me is Jim Bouton's *Ball Four.*

I stumbled onto *Ball Four* at a church yard sale when I was about ten years old, give or take a year. I was still playing

Little League, and still had the dream many kids have at that age of being a star athlete when I grew up, although I already sort of knew that wasn't really going to happen. Still, I read everything about sports I could get my hands on. (I remember I also picked up an old copy of George Plimpton's *Paper Lion* at that yard sale, too.)

My mom just saw a book that was obviously about baseball and didn't ask any questions. In retrospect, she probably should have, because ten years old was way too young for me to learn about all the rampant misogyny and drug and alcohol use that fueled Major League Baseball in 1969. It was basically the equivalent of stumbling onto an R-rated movie on cable and watching it on my own. Of course, I thought it was great—and I held on to Bouton's tell-it-like-it-is, warts-and-all voice as a model for how to write about yourself and the people around you well into adulthood.

(I never read *Harriet the Spy* as a kid—but when I finally did, in my forties, I realized the same lessons people say they learned from that novel about how the world reacts when you tell the truth I had learned from *Ball Four*. Except that Jim Bouton didn't apologize, and wasn't fully forgiven by baseball loyalists until much later in life, if at all. As a result, my takeaway on people hating you for what you write was: "Good. That means you're doing it right.")

I reread *Ball Four* a couple years ago, and reading it as a middle-aged adult is a much different experience than reading it as a precocious tween. What stuck with me this time around was the portrait of Bouton at thirty, scrambling to hold on to his place in baseball, just looking to make the roster on a newly created expansion team, and coming to understand that he'd taken his unique asset—the ability to throw a knuckleball—

about as far as he could, and the ride was about to end, and he had no idea what he was supposed to do next.

In that sense, what a preadolescent boy had seen as a wild, raunchy account of life in the big leagues was actually a stark account of . . . well, Bouton was too young to call it a midlife crisis, I suppose, but also too far along in his professional career to describe it as a "quarter-life crisis" (which didn't exist as a concept then, anyway).

Ball Four is a memoir that I would recommend to anyone grappling with the prospect of writing about themselves— only now, instead of saying that it's because Jim Bouton taught me you have to be honest enough to include everything, even the stuff that's going to upset the people around you, I'd tell you that it's because he was unafraid to write honestly about his most vulnerable, insecure moments.

You could even say that *Ball Four* changed my life twice.

There's no guarantee that you'll be able to change someone else's life with your book, let alone change it twice. But who is the one person whose life your writing is guaranteed to change? The answer, of course, is *you*.

Remember the goal that Thomas Merton established? "Learning who one is, and learning what one has to offer to the contemporary world, and then learning how to make that offering valid." A consistent writing practice, like a consistent meditation practice, or a consistent prayer practice, can help you get through that learning process with a greater sense of clarity and purpose.

As you write, as you learn to tap into your thoughts and dreams and concerns, you start to realize what *really* matters to you, the things that are so precious that you can't help but share them with the world. Writing gives you the tools to identify the most profound aspects of yourself *and* to bring them forward without restraint. You lay it out on the page, and you declare, "This is what matters to me. This is what I care about. I want you to care about it, too."

Then, fingers crossed, somebody finds what you've written, and it persuades them to care.

To bring this back to *A Christmas Carol*, I don't know how writing that story changed Charles Dickens's life, though I'm curious to find out, and if I get a chance one day, I should crack open a biography and see if it sheds any light on the subject. What I do know without doing any research is this: *A Christmas Carol* works because Dickens believed every word he wrote. It's not a cynical commercial ploy; it's a sincere testament of how Christmas is inextricably bound to notions of charity and compassion and repentance.

One of the things I love about watching the film every year is that Alastair Sim's performance makes it clear that Scrooge chooses to be an asshole to the rest of the world not because he's unfeeling, but because *he has felt deeply*. Scrooge no longer trusts joy because in his experience, it has always been followed by trauma, and if the absence of joy in his life is the price he has to pay to evade trauma, he's willing to wade through the constant dull misery. Once the Christmas ghosts start in on him, Scrooge acknowledges quickly that he made the wrong call—the evening is largely spent tearing down his objections that it's *too late* for him to find redemption. But Dickens believed that it was never too late.

What is it, then, you believe as strongly as Dickens believed that? If you don't know yet, keep writing. Your writing is an opportunity to make a statement. Be sure that what you're saying means something to you.

I was watching a PBS documentary about the painter Mark Rothko, which about halfway through the film cites a letter he co-wrote with Adolph Gottlieb in 1943 after the *New York Times* gave an exhibition of their work an unenthusiastic review. "To us," Rothko and Gottlieb wrote, ". . . art is an adventure into an unknown world, which can be explored only by those willing to take the risks."

The idea that this process of discovery can only be undertaken "by those willing to take the risks" may seem elitist—but, as I've come to understand it over the years, *any of us* are capable of taking that risk. We only have to make the affirmative decision to do so. It's true that the way the world works on a day-to-day basis can persuade many of us that we don't have the power to make that decision: We have too many responsibilities; we don't have enough time; we probably wouldn't be any good at it . . . you've heard these rationalizations before. You've probably laid them upon yourself at some point.

But you picked this book up because there's a still, small voice inside you that believes there's another possibility, a better possibility. Let's listen to *that* voice for a while. As Rothko and Gottlieb said in their letter: "This world of the imagination is fancy-free and violently opposed to common sense."

I look at this statement in two ways. First, I recognize that the decision to dedicate yourself to a creative practice, whether it's painting or writing or something else, is almost never a "common sense" decision. Like I said above, the world offers plenty of "sensible" reasons *not* to pursue a creative practice, to just slot yourself into the system and do the normal, expected, *safe* thing. Even after you make the decision to pursue a creative life, you might find yourself fighting off doubt, whether it's your own internal misgivings or people around you who are convinced that you're not going to make it.

But you're going to try anyway, you're going to embark on this reckless adventure, and with any luck, it's going to be a liberating process. (And, honestly, even if you "fail," it's still likely to be liberating in certain ways.)

Second, let's look at this statement *within* our creative practice. Are we looking to tell ourselves what we already know? Of course not. We're looking to learn *new* things, and that means we need to be willing to look in new places, to make unexpected choices.

Even if you're writing the realest of realist fiction imaginable, at some point you'll need to stop thinking about what *should* happen in your story and open yourself up to what *could* happen. Take chances, make guesses, follow instincts. If you write yourself into a corner, work your way back and try a different path!

Just as you didn't start writing to tell yourself what you already know, you aren't writing to tell other readers what *they* already know, either. As Rothko and Gottlieb said, "It is our functions as artists to make the spectator see the world our way—not his way." So let's fall back on the fundamental questions: What is it that you're most compelled to share with the rest of the world? What is the thing that gives your writing purpose? What is the story you *need* to tell?

Satisfy those demands, and readers will ultimately follow you.

Some people might argue that you need to play to readers' expectations if you expect to keep their attention—and there's an extent to which that's true. As an obvious example, if you're writing a romance novel, it had better end with two people in love or you *will* catch hell from readers. But that doesn't mean that you have to mechanically follow convention from start to finish. It doesn't mean you have to populate your story with stock characters; it doesn't mean you have to stick to an outline of conventional scenes that take your lovers from their first meeting to the final clinch.

If conventional scenes are meaningful to you, go ahead and write those scenes. But if you find your characters making unconventional choices, run with them. Write a story that convinces *you* with its emotional authenticity, that says something *you* believe to be true about the world, and the force of your belief will carry the story. If the characters feel real to you, if they aren't just going through the motions, they will feel real to readers.

(I'm not just talking about romance anymore, either.)

———————

Here's another example from the art world that gets at what I'm trying to say: I once saw a documentary called *The Lost Bird Project* about the sculptor Todd McGrain and his efforts to create memorials to bird species that once flourished in North America and have become extinct since Europeans came and settled the continent. He creates statues that capture the birds' form, then installs them near the places where those birds were last seen before dying out—a heath hen, for example, by the side of a road in a state forest on Martha's Vineyard.

At one point in the film, McGrain talks about how creating the statues is only one facet of the "project." His work isn't complete until he figures out where to place the statues—and that involves going out and talking to other people, trying to convince them to allow him to put six-foot bronze sculptures on their land. This is new, uncomfortable territory for him, he explains, because it forces him to get out of the studio and sell himself and his work in ways that he hadn't really had to face before. Which, in turn, requires him to be able to talk about his work—to explain *why* he wants us to remember these birds, and *why* these public memorials are an effective way to get people thinking about what's been lost, and at what cost.

Once, when I was teaching a one-day workshop on how to pitch yourself to agents and editors, one of the writers had voiced her frustrations with the whole process of pitches and query letters. She'd spent all this time finding and honing her artistic voice, she said, and now she couldn't even let that work speak for itself; she had to learn a whole new way of talking about it.

I totally understand that frustration, and frankly, there are still times when I have trouble articulating my current works-in-progress. You spend weeks, months, even years thinking about a story or a concept. It takes up a good-sized chunk of mental real estate as you become intimately familiar with all of its facets, meticulously working over each detail until everything interlaces just so. And then you have to figure out how to describe that work in two or three sentences, not just to pitch it to an agent or editor, but even just to answer the question: "So, what are you writing about?"

I can tell you what I told those writers about the three questions a good pitch answers: *Who/what is this about? What's at stake? Why does it matter?* But those questions are just my framing of the fundamental process of being able to tell *yourself* what you're doing as a writer (or any sort of creative person) and why you're doing it. The closer you can come to that kind of clarity and self-knowledge, the easier the work becomes—and the more opportunity you have to expand upon it. Once you do one thing you've set out to do, you'll start to see how many ways you might be able to build upon that accomplishment.

One of the reasons I was so moved by *The Lost Bird Project* is that it's clear Todd McGrain finds a joyful reward in convincing strangers in five different communities, from Florida to Nova Scotia, to accept the gift of his art—and in so doing, to share their own history with the world. He found the story that he wanted to tell in bronze and learned how to describe it in ways that convinced other people it was a story that needed to be told.

I'm not saying that finding your story will save you from ever having to flail around again to figure out what you're writing. Stories or nonfictional themes rarely fall into our laps fully formed. But the process of exploration becomes . . . well, if not necessarily *easier*, then perhaps a bit less anxiety-provoking if we know going in that we're here because there's *something* we want to share with the world, something to which we're already intuitively connected, and that all we need to do now is give it time.

Chapter Three:

Our Endless and Proper Work

Conan O'Brien's first late-night talk show debuted on NBC in the fall of 1993. I was a young graduate student, of an age where I thought nothing of staying up until 1:30 in the morning, especially when I'd arranged my life so I usually didn't have to be anywhere until noon at the earliest. He had a great deal of fun playing with the conventions of late-night TV, and I became an instant fan. Although my enthusiasm eventually tapered off, especially during a period of several years when I didn't own a television, I tried to keep up with the highlights—when he finally took over *The Tonight Show*, for example, and when NBC unceremoniously took that show back from him to appease Jay Leno, which prompted O'Brien to start a new show on cable.

That show, *Conan*, started out in the same vein as *Late Night with Conan O'Brien* and *The Tonight Show*. There was an opening monologue, after which he'd move to his desk and do another comedy bit with Andy Richter, then interview a celebrity, then do a halftime comedy bit, then another celebrity interview, and maybe a musical guest.

In 2018, though, O'Brien decided to shake things up. He cut the show down to a half hour, ditched the desk, and even dropped the live band that used to play guests onto the set and cover the segues to commercial.

"I was the new guy for so long, and then that card flips overnight—you go from the inexperienced, nervous punk

37

to the old dean emeritus," O'Brien told a *New York Times* journalist about the changes. "I started to think, does it have to be that way? Let's say I've got a couple years left in me. What if I tried to, in the most selfish way possible, alter this so that I have a maximum amount of fun?"

As a writer, I loved that idea. We all run the risk of writing ourselves into a groove—which may actually be reasonably profitable, if it turns out to be a groove that readers like, but even that can come at a psychological cost. "I know when I've been feeling like we're padding out the show because I've got to get to the full hour," O'Brien said. "When I know that the part of the show that has the real protein and that people really want, happened in the first half-hour—literally the first twenty-one, twenty-two minutes."

That second half of the show wasn't sparking joy, so he threw it out. Then, in late 2020, he reinvented his creative process yet again, announcing that he would wind down his late-night cable talk show and develop a weekly variety series for the HBO Max streaming service.

I realize how ridiculous it sounds to tell you, "Every time you sit down to write, it should feel like an adventure." You and I both know that's not going to happen. Even when we love what we're writing, there will be days when it feels like a chore, a grinding slog. In the long run, though, if our writing is the means by which we figure out who we are, and what we have to share with the world, that process of discovery *should* feel like an adventure. Some days you have to hack through the forest; some days you have to wade hip-deep in the mud, but it's worth it for those days when you can stand at the mountain peak or look out over the coastline.

Part of that adventure involves pushing ourselves into new territory. I'm not saying you have to emulate Conan O'Brien's example by throwing away a voice you've developed through years of hard work and taking up an entirely new style. Just for kicks, though: What is it about your writing that you've never been fully satisfied by, but have come to accept as a necessary burden? Try leaving that out of your next project—either find another way to produce the same effect, or just drop it and see where the new approach takes you.

Do you feel like you're working the same territory over and over again in your writing? What would you like to write about but have convinced yourself you can't, because you're not ready, or because it's not what people expect from you? Pick that up for a while and play with it.

You may be familiar with Mary Oliver's one particularly famous injunction, from "The Summer Day": "Tell me, what is it you plan to do with your one wild and precious life?" But I'm drawn to a line from another of her poems, "Yes! No!":

"To pay attention, this is our endless and proper work."

"Yes! No!" clearly situates that dictum in the context of the natural world, but it's *not* about going out into the woods or the fields and merely observing what happens around you. If it were, Oliver wouldn't have also said, "I think serenity is not something you just find in the world, like a plum tree, holding up its white petals," and she wouldn't have advised us that "imagination is better than a sharp instrument."

Pay attention to what happens around you, for sure, but also pay attention to what it stirs within you, because that's where you will find yourself. And if you're having trouble finding yourself, give some thought to *how* and *where* you're looking, and don't be afraid of changing one or the other . . . or both.

———————

Like a lot of people, I was moved by Hannah Gadsby's Netflix special, *Nanette*, a show that started out as your standard stand-up comedy hour but gradually shifted, by way of a feminist critique of art history and a deconstruction of the entire premise of stand-up comedy, into a passionate attack on . . . when I say "patriarchy" or "Western civilization," that makes it sound grandiose; on the other hand, "the way things are" sounds too vague. Let's just say Gadbsy has been enduring the effects of misogyny and homophobia pretty much all her life, and a key element of *Nanette* is her excavation and explanation of just how deep they've penetrated into her psyche.

It's a powerful hour of television, and if you have Netflix and you haven't pulled it up yet, you should make some time for it.

One of the things I found fascinating as I watched *Nanette* was its "meta" aspects—like, as I mentioned before, Gadsby's deconstruction of the stand-up form. Stand-up comedy is about creating tension, then dissolving that tension with a joke, over and over again. The audience feels anxious, but a funny quip gives them an escape hatch, an opportunity to relax, only to be made anxious again, and rewarded with a bigger release . . . but, as Gadsby points out, the comedian is the one who's making them feel anxious in the first place. "I made you tense," she tells the crowd. "This is an abusive relationship."

She had become fed up with that—and fed up with telling jokes about herself that reinforced the negative self-image a homophobic society had drilled into her. ("When I came out of the closet," she says, "the only thing I was allowed to do was to be invisible and hate myself.") And so, less than halfway into her performance, she announces that she's finished with comedy, and then, over the course of the next half-hour or so, she begins to strip away the jokes. Oh, there's still laughs to be found for a while, but they taper off, until the last quarter of the show is completely serious, denying the audience any cathartic release.

As a writer, one of the things that captivates me in Gadsby's performance—beyond the things that she's actually saying—is the way she dramatizes the realization that she had something to tell the world and the moment she understood the way she'd chosen to do it wasn't working. Now, a big part of that is Gadsby understanding and accepting that the version of herself she *had* been sharing with the world through her stand-up routines was no longer who she wanted to be, no longer who she wanted to present herself as being—in fact, it was a self-destructive persona she could no longer afford to be.

But then, as she began to comprehend who she really wanted to be, and zeroed in on the message she really wanted to share with her audiences, she discovered stand-up comedy didn't provide a framework capable of adequately communicating that new identity. She needed to come up with a new delivery system, a new way of speaking—even at the risk of it being a format that audiences might not find welcoming.

Think about that for a moment. The concert hall-sized audience for *Nanette* came expecting a stand-up comedy special, and they got that for a little while. And then they found themselves in something more akin to a Spalding Gray monologue, which in turn gave way to something with the topical urgency and earnestness of a TED talk. In the hands of a lesser speaker—a lesser writer—it's very easy to imagine the audience rejecting this unfamiliar, unwelcome new thing. But Gadsby held it together by, among other things, sheer force of personality. She kept them with her all the way to the end. And, in the process, she transitioned in the public eye from being an accomplished comedian to something even more distinctive and still slightly undefinable.

Some writers find their groove early on, and they're able to work comfortably in that zone for the rest of their lives. For other writers, though, a moment may come when the story you want to tell next just doesn't fit into your familiar genre. I know a fantastic romance author, for example, who started writing psychological thrillers a few years ago, and it's opened up whole new avenues for her to use her protagonists to talk about society from a feminist perspective. (Her name's Victoria Helen Stone. I'm biased, but her books are really good.)

If you find yourself in a situation where the old, familiar ways you've honed of telling a story are no longer working for you, you can try to figure out how to force the story into working the usual way . . . or you can sit with it a while longer see if you can find another way to tell it. You might even realize the story you thought you wanted to tell isn't actually the one you want to tell. It'll mean a lot more work, and you may have to push yourself into some uncomfortable places to get it done.

If you have any doubts about whether it'll be worth doing, though, just take a look at *Nanette*. Or—if you'll pardon a very abrupt change of subject—you could read *Secret Body: Erotic and Esoteric Currents in the History of Religions* by Jeffrey Kripal, a professor at Rice University.

I first learned about Kripal's work about seven years ago, when he wrote a book called *Mutants and Mystics* that deals with the ways comic books and science fiction stories have addressed paranormal experiences—a natural fit for someone like me, whose adolescence was punctuated by Alan Moore's *Swamp Thing* comics and the novels of Philip K. Dick. As an intellectual memoir of Kripal's academic career, *Secret Body* addresses some of that material, but it also covers all the other things he's been studying over the decades.

Here's the quick tour: After attempting to become a teenage ascetic, Kripal enrolled in a Catholic seminary and eventually realized not just that he was one of the few heterosexual men in his class, but that the priestly spiritual life, the relationship between the priest and God, seemed to require a homoerotic mysticism that he simply couldn't muster. So he became an academic, found a focus in the history of religions, and became particularly interested in the writings of Ramakrishna Paramahamsa, a nineteenth-century Hindu spiritual leader, one of the first such gurus to whom the West was widely exposed.

It turned out that the English-language editions of Ramakrishna were heavily redacted, so Kripal dug into the original texts, discovering a strong homoerotic strain that had been suppressed for more than a century. He wrote about it in his first book, *Kali's Child*, and was promptly attacked by Hindu nationalists in India, who accused him of attempting to smear their religion. This conflict was drawn out for so long that eventually, Kripal moved into other fields of research just to get away from it.

We need to backtrack a bit, though, because while Kripal was in India doing that early research, something happened to him. "That Night," as he calls it, when "although my body was asleep . . . [my] consciousness was lucid and clear, fully awake," and "a powerful electric-like energy flooded the body with wave after wave of an unusually deep and uniform arousal," until "I felt my 'I' being sucked up into an ecstasy that felt entirely too much like a death."

He's never had an experience like that again, he explains, and yet it served as the spur that would eventually lead him to write *Mutants and Mystics*, along with several other books that touch upon American culture's relationship to science, religion, and mystical or paranormal experiences.

Mind you, I'm reading all this as someone who came of age at a time when the paranormal left an especially outsized imprint on pop culture, and as someone who has also had unusual experiences, although nothing quite as intense as That Night. So I'm attracted to the gravity Kripal invests in the subject matter, but I also appreciate how he is able to look back at his work and identify the common threads—how he's able to recognize that, while his attention was drawn to new areas over the years, it was actually all part of a process of learning more about what it is he's been drawn to share. And he turned that self-discovery into a challenge to his fellow religious historians to reimagine their field for the twenty-first century.

You might not have experienced anything as drastic and dramatic as That Night, either, but consider this: Have you ever found yourself drawn to a new story, one that seems at odds with the type of stories you've been working on until that moment? Or gotten such intensely negative criticism for something that you've written that you decided you would never tackle that subject matter again? Or had someone point out that several stories you were sure showed how versatile you were as a writer actually had a fairly obvious common theme?

Those can be frightening or depressing scenarios . . . but they don't *have* to be. You can embrace the challenge of diving into new territory, learning new things about the world but also new things about yourself. And when self-discovery compels us to change our lives, our writing will by necessity change as well. Again, you might not necessarily feel a wave of cosmic energy overtake your consciousness, but your creative spirit will steer you toward the things that will help you become the storyteller you want to be—even if you don't fully understand what that entails at the beginning. Some of us may figure it out as we're going about our work, and some of us may only realize where we were headed once we get there.

Ultimately, though, I think the early flash of inspiration and the late dawn of realization are both less significant than the process itself. Even the days when the writing doesn't go well, when you can't quite figure out how to say what you want to say, are necessary steps toward the day when you will have something you're ready to share.

———————

Along those lines, I want to tell you about Bettina Rodriguez Aguilera, a woman who sought the Republican nomination in the race for a House seat in Miami back in 2018. She had an endorsement from the *Miami Herald*, but it came with a caveat—she took all the right stands for a would-be Republican congresswoman, the editors at her local paper said. You just had to overlook the fact that, several years earlier, she had gone on Spanish-language television and described how she'd been abducted by aliens when she was a child and had been in intermittent telepathic contact with them for some time afterward. Set that aside, they said, and she's a very sensible Republican at heart.

You can imagine the merriment that ensued on social media.

For her own part, Rodriguez Aguilera was careful to say that her childhood encounter with aliens was real but didn't define her, and that she wanted voters to consider her positions and her track record in local politics—exactly the right stand to take under the circumstances, I thought. You might have your own opinion as to the validity of Rodriguez Aguilera's account. Clearly *something* happened to her as a child, though, and this is how she has framed it. As long as she wasn't claiming her political ideology was handed down to her by the aliens, I didn't see any need to challenge her story. (If I lived in her district, I wouldn't have voted for her anyway, though, because I'm not a Republican.)

Even after Rodriguez Aguilera lost her primary, I kept thinking about how we have stories to tell—in many cases, stories to tell *about ourselves*—and as much as we would like the world to see those stories the way we see them, we can't control other people's responses. A memoir, for example, can be seen as an effort to guide others to what you believe is the "correct reading" of your life, but you're always going to encounter someone who looks at the same set of facts, ignores your interpretation, and sees it through their own lens.

They won't just *see* it through their own lens, though. They'll *talk* about how they see it—and, these days, that means you need to be prepared to see other people talking about your memoir (or whatever kind of book you write, for that matter) in ways you think are just *wrong*. If you can't wrap your head around that possibility, if you can't stand the idea that somebody out there isn't going to share your vision, then perhaps you aren't quite as ready to share that vision as you think you are.

Bettina Rodriguez Aguilera knew that *most* people would likely side-eye her over the alien abduction thing, but she didn't let that stop her from being the political candidate she wanted to be, the candidate she was convinced she could be—and, ultimately, the candidate the *Miami Herald* recognized she could be, too. For all my political differences with her, I'm impressed with the way she owned and took charge of her story.

I'm also impressed with the way actor Geoffrey Owens took charge of *his* story not long after Rodriguez Aguilera had faded from the headlines. You might remember Owens as Dr. Huxtable's son-in-law from *The Cosby Show*. He's had his ups and downs as a professional actor since that sitcom gig, and by 2018, he was working part-time at a Trader Joe's in New Jersey to make ends meet. A customer recognized him, snapped some pictures with her smartphone, then sent them to the *Daily Mail*, and from there they ended up on the Fox News website as well.

That initial "coverage" had a distinctly vicious glee to it, standard "look at the washed-up celebrity" stuff. A lot of people refused to accept that framing, however, calling Fox News, the *Daily Mail*, and the original customer out on their efforts to humiliate Owens. Professional actors came forward and testified to how hard it can be to scrape by between gigs; working-class people were rightfully infuriated at the characterization of grocery store work as shameful. It only took a few days for sympathetic media outlets to invite

Owens to talk about how he took the job to pay the bills, how he specifically liked working at Trader Joe's because it gave him the flexibility to keep pursuing acting gigs, and how he'd actually been recognized just about every day he worked there—it's just that most people showed more class about it.

In one interview, when he was asked if he hoped that all the attention would get him some acting jobs, he said he hoped it might get him some *auditions*, but that he didn't want to be cast in a project out of sympathy—he wanted to be cast because he was the right actor for the part. (He ended up landing supporting roles on two TV shows, which was nice, because an unfortunate side effect of all the publicity was that he could no longer work effectively at the Trader Joe's and had to leave the job.)

Geoffrey Owens wasn't even trying to tell a story about himself; he was just keeping his head down, doing the best he could, when somebody decided to tell a story about him. But he rose to meet that story head-on because he had a different story he could tell, and he wouldn't let somebody else's story shake him.

I admire both Owens and Rodriguez Aguilera for their conviction, and I'll keep it in mind the next time I put something I've written out in the world and people start layering meanings onto it that I never intended, including some meanings I *specifically* didn't intend. That's not to say that we can't *ever* learn from what other people tell us about our own stories—but if you know what you're here to do, and you're doing it, you don't have to worry when somebody doesn't get it. You just have to believe that someone else will.

Chapter Four:

Reclaiming Your Time for Writing

I was at a writer's conference once, and during the Q&A session, a woman asked me about maintaining your creative focus on an ongoing basis. How do you make the ongoing decision to write rather than not write, especially when the world offers you so many enticing (or simply overwhelming) alternatives to writing?

It was a great question, because there wasn't an easy answer. It's one thing to say, for example, "I'm going to write for an hour tonight instead of watching that TV show." It's another thing entirely to say, "I'm going to write for an hour tonight instead of worrying that the world is falling apart."

I know a lot of other writers who, to one degree or another, have been frustrated—not necessarily creatively derailed, but hindered to say the least—by the distractions we all face these days. I was able to tell the woman at that workshop about mindfulness techniques that have worked for me over the years, ways of recalibrating my attention away from the distractions and back toward writing the thing I want to share with the world. I also put in a good word for therapy—long after my therapist and I had basically agreed I had a level of anxiety roughly appropriate to the state of the world, it was extremely helpful to be able to spend forty-five minutes unloading the stuff that had built up in my head over the last week to someone who could give me meaningful feedback.

I also remembered to tell the audience at that workshop that sometimes you *do* need to lean into the distraction. You need things to come together at work, you need your relationship to work out, you need to make sure you and your loved ones can enjoy a healthy life together. That doesn't make you a bad writer; it just means you don't have time to write *at the moment.*

Learning to tell the difference between a situation that needs to be addressed and a distraction that can be set aside is . . . well, look, I can't tell you I've got a perfect solution to that. I have, however, gotten better at dealing with *some* of the little distractions.

My iPhone, for example, has an app called Screen Time that sends me an alert every Sunday morning, once it's generated a report on how much time I've spent on the device every day and how much of that time goes to specific apps.

I looked at the data the first few weeks after I got the app, so I would learn, for example, that my overall usage one week was down 25 percent from the week before, although I still wasn't exactly excited about how much of that time I was spending on social media, and I had thought I was spending more time reading ebooks than the numbers showed.

I'd like to count some of those hours as "writing time," like when I was reading articles to research something I was writing, or when I was following some associative mental threads sparked by something I'd read on Twitter. But that only allows me to rationalize some moments, and it leaves a whole bunch of time where I was definitely *not* writing.

I don't bring this up to flagellate myself—at least, not for very long. It's just a reminder that a writing practice is grounded in conscious choices, and that what you get from your writing practice is determined by what you put into it. "If you possess so much as a mustard seed of faith," Jesus said, "you will say to this mountain, 'Move from here to there,' and it will move, and nothing will be impossible to you."

To me, that's a message about *focus* and *concentration* and *intention*. Most of us live our lives pulled in a thousand different directions by a thousand different distractions, but we know from experience that when we apply ourselves to a particular task, when we train ourselves to perform it well and then go out and do it, it gets done. Our writing practices are a perfect example of that.

The problem, as I said, is that the universe conspires to pull us in a thousand different directions away from our writing.

Okay, I admit, *conspires* is a loaded word; it's not as if the universe is consciously acting to thwart you in your dreams of becoming a writer. And not all of the distractions life throws in our path are so awful.

But I'm talking about the ways in which we're told, starting when we're very young, that writing (like other creative pursuits) isn't *practical*, that we should be looking ahead to a *real job*, to a *career*. We're trained from childhood to show up at certain places, at certain times, to do *this* assignment for *these* people by *that* date or suffer the consequences, which might include not getting into *the right school* that will set us up for that *real job*.

So you get that job, and then you've got to be out the door early enough to make the commute to get to your office and do more assignments for more people, then make the commute back home. You might still want to develop a writing practice around that, but the social media beckons, and so does the streaming entertainment, and they all eat into your time, and you've got to be in bed at a decent hour so you can get enough sleep to get up early tomorrow and do it all again. You do what you can, but you find yourself wondering if it will ever be enough.

———

Perhaps the universe doesn't conspire to keep us from becoming writers, but society sure seems to do its best to discourage us. But what if we found a different organizing principle around which to build our daily schedules?

Am I saying you should quit your job and devote yourself to writing full-time? Well, I'm not saying *not* to do that, but I have to admit it's not a very practical decision, unless you've got some kind of support structure lined up—which seems more unlikely than ever these days.

You *can* start reclaiming your time, minute by minute. Start with the distractions outside the office: How much television do you really need to watch? Are you reading for edification, or escape? How many people do you really need to follow on Facebook or Twitter or Instagram? Are all those follows really strengthening your relationships, or are they your means of escape?

I remember reading once about something called "Dunbar's number," the theoretical maximum number of relationships one can maintain and still be capable of engaging meaningfully with everyone without being overwhelmed. Robin Dunbar suggests this number is around 150, but on Twitter, I've cut it down to 93.

I'm slightly less stringent when it comes to Facebook, but that's partially because I don't really use Facebook to stay in close contact with people. As I've joked to friends, it's basically a website I have to deal with in order to see pictures of my nephews.

Bear with me for a second, as I want to share something Wendell Berry said in a recent *New Yorker* profile:

> We really have to turn against the selfishness of the individualism that sees everybody as a competitor of everybody else. When we see how destructive that is, and we turn against it, then we have our life's work.

Of all the practical life lessons we could draw from that statement, I want to focus on social media. It's become conventional wisdom for writers, wherever they happen to be on the publication spectrum, that they need to use social media to connect with their readers. *How else are you going to get noticed? Don't you want readers to find you?* I've been as guilty of touting that line as anybody else over the last decade—along with my standard caveat that you can't just use social media as a megaphone to promote your wares, you have to authentically "engage" with people. Frankly, though, that's not all *that* innovative a twist.

I still believe social media is an extension of ourselves, and that as our writing practice grows, and through that practice we gain a better understanding of ourselves, we can use social media to communicate that understanding in profound ways—and, yes, among the other consequences of doing so, we might possibly gain readers.

What I want to challenge, though, starting from Wendell Berry's edict of removing ourselves from competition with the rest of the world, is the notion that you or I could be "better" or "worse" at social media than some other writers. I know I've gone through the stage where I compared my follower count on Twitter to other writers' and wondered what I could do to boost mine even higher—and even after I stopped comparing myself directly to everyone else, I'd still try to figure out how I could reach some arbitrary milestone that was just out of reach.

The other key aspect of "popularity" on social media is how often your content is appreciated—and even though I've managed to put the concern with my follower count behind me, I can still obsess over whether a tweet I've written is being retweeted or liked. I'll write something I'm sure will go viral, then keep checking my notifications page to see how much attention it gets. Even though, intellectually, I know it's a total crapshoot, I'll still feel a twinge of frustration when a tweet I thought was particularly clever doesn't take off.

I've tried to work past that, by closing the tab in my smartphone's browser dedicated to my Twitter notifications page, but I haven't been able to shake the habit for good yet. According to conventional social media wisdom, I probably *should* be paying attention to likes and retweets to see "what's working," so I can fine-tune my social media presentation to be more resonant with my readership blah blah blah . . . but instead of focusing on what the world would *like* me to be, I'd rather focus on who I *need* to *become*.

I'm not saying you should abandon social media. It still has potential to be a powerful vehicle for personal expression—and you should also open yourself to the possibility of meaningful dialogue. What I'm hoping is that there's a way to do that without getting caught up in expectations of success, especially not success as measured by the benchmarks Twitter (and Facebook and Instagram and all the other platforms) set up to hook us into playing their game by their rules.

An aspiring author once went on Twitter to complain about how her agent had submitted a book proposal to four editors, and three of them rejected her, claiming her social media platform wasn't "big enough" to "make a splash . . . in the crowded market." From experience, I can confirm that book publishing is, for the most part, a risk-averse industry, and a large social media following allows publishers to feel slightly more comfortable about acquiring a book, just as sales figures for previous books might, if they exist. Nothing is guaranteed, of course, but they can tell themselves the numbers are there! The potential audience exists! It should work!

The problem is that agents and writers inevitably end up buying into that premise that the ultimate goal is *more*—more followers, more likes, more retweets, more shares—as well. In our efforts to expand our platforms, however, we risk losing sight of the real reason to be on social media—to cultivate authentic connections with other people on the strength of the passions we reveal through our writing.

There's a passage in John Eldredge's *Restoration Year* that speaks very clearly to the problem with pursuing social media "success." All too often, in the quest to become popular, we're willing to play to the audience, to behave in slightly (or not so slightly) inauthentic ways because we think it'll get us noticed.

Once you start down that path, it can be difficult to turn back. As Eldredge writes:

> The awful burden of the false self is that it must be constantly maintained. You believe you have to keep doing something in order to be desirable. Once you

find something that brings you attention, you have to keep it going, or risk the loss of attention.

Stop worrying whether what you tweet or post "resonates" with people in oh-so-easily quantifiable ways. That doesn't mean you should use social media simply as a broadcast tool to bombard people with announcements about what you're doing or what you've got for sale; it means you should concern yourself with more substantial *responses*. Does what you write move people to tell you *why* it moved them, to explain in their own words *why* they're sharing with their friends? Does it inspire them to initiate a conversation? Do their responses prompt you to delve deeper into the things that concern you most, rather than going for an easy hot take?

If the version of you that shows up on social media is consistently true to the person who's being shaped by your writing practice, that authenticity will come through in what you write, and people will pay *real* attention. And some of those people will want to pay attention to what you write outside social media, if it's available for them to read. You'll know, because they'll tell you. Instead of attempting to go viral, look for those responses. And if a publisher tells you your work is interesting but your platform isn't big enough, recognize what's underneath that statement: "I might want to publish you, but I'm not confident I'll be able to get it right, and I'm not comfortable taking the chance."

Focus on being yourself online. Don't try to flood the zone; just show up when you have something to say. I can't guarantee being consistently authentic will bring you a wave of followers, but I can guarantee that it will put you on the path to being a consistently better writer.

Along those lines, I once read a tweet by television and comic book writer Bryan Edward Hill that reinforces what I've been saying *and* pivots in a slightly different direction:

> Snark Wars on Twitter are fine and all, but make sure most of your energy is dedicated to practicing your chosen craft and building alliances. You can't pay rent with the endorphin rush of social media. If something isn't making you money, it's likely costing you some.

People latched on to that last sentence and accused Hill of having a mercenary attitude, so he returned to Twitter to clarify what he'd meant. "I do many things that don't *directly* bring in revenue," he wrote, "but they all secure my peace of mind . . . which makes it easier for me to do things that do bring in revenue. The mind is unified, everything affects it. . . . If something isn't adding to your productivity, then it's taking away from it."

Now, I love me a good snark war on Twitter; it can be a helpful way to release some of the frustration I've felt over our political and cultural miseries. Yet I'm also mindful (some days more than others) that clever put-downs aren't necessarily that helpful to me or to society in the long run. I'm not so much worried about it affecting my social media "brand," but I do try to make sure that when I do get into those discussions, I'm making an effort to clarify my beliefs and, when I can, to steer readers toward other people who have relevant wisdom to share. I fall short of that goal often, but I keep trying.

———————

I firmly believe that the writing life is something we work at even when we're not sitting at our keyboard or with our pen in hand, that it's something we should strive to be focused on continually and consistently. "What do you want from writing?" I ask audiences when I talk at literary conferences and workshops. "And what are you doing that gets in the way of achieving that?" How are you wasting time and energy that could be better applied toward your writing—and what prevents you from abandoning those wasteful practices?

That isn't a cutthroat command to "always be working," though. As I conceded when I tweeted about Hill's message, "We all have to go off the clock *sometimes*." But I also immediately qualified that statement to say that when we do go off the clock, it's "not in ways that'll throw us off our game come game time."

I spend a *lot* of my non writing time reading, but it's all (even when it's just for fun) with a glimmer of hope that it'll make me a better writer. I also do a lot of things that I hope will ground me, make me a calmer, more reflective person, whether it's taking time out to play with my cats or spending Sunday mornings at Quaker meetings. I also try to be mindful about how much television I let into my life, although, let me tell you, that one's *hard*. You set out to watch *one* nature documentary on the DVR and before you know it, you're absorbed in an all-night string of competitions between amateur weapon makers . . .

But, you know, that's okay, too. Or, at least, I'm not going to beat myself up *too* badly over it. We're not writing machines, after all. The key is *intention*: If you're willing to continually apply yourself to your writing, even after you've seemingly fallen short of the mark, you'll have something to show for your work eventually. And, perhaps, every time you pick yourself up after having a setback reduces the likelihood of falling into that same trap again. (*Reduces*, not *eliminates*. Again, we're not machines.)

Once you decide to reclaim your time, try to bundle it together as best you can, and set those chunks of time aside for writing. Then write. You're not going to be moving mountains right away—still, maybe you'll notice that you're beginning to feel more at ease with yourself. Any doubts and insecurities you might have about your writing won't necessarily vanish—I suspect they never do, not entirely, not even if you're hugely successful—but every day you build on your writing practice is a day that will strengthen your belief in that practice.

Let's bring this back full circle and talk about one of Bryan Edward Hill's projects: *Black Lightning/Hong Kong Phooey*. I was genuinely excited to hear about this comic book—more excited than I had been about any comic in about fifteen years—precisely because it's such a ridiculous idea on the surface. And in the hands of a lesser writer, potentially problematic—the original Hong Kong Phooey, a staple of 1970s Saturday morning television, was a literally cartoonish appropriation of Asian culture in the form of a canine martial arts master.

The more I heard about it, though, the more intriguing it sounded—you got a sense that Hill was taking some formative influences and giving them a truly personal creative spin. His gleefully uncontained excitement about getting to work on a comic book with the artist Denys Cowan was also a big selling point for me, because I'm just a few years older than Hill, and therefore also a comics fan who came of age in the '80s, for whom the name Denys Cowan invokes an instant "YES, PLEASE."

In an interview about the book, Hill talked about how he came up with the original idea, something in the spirit of 1970s Black action and Hong Kong martial arts movies, but was told that his story was undoable. Much later, he had an opportunity to pitch DC Comics as part of a project where their superheroes would team up with Hanna-Barbera cartoon characters, and he gave them a different, more subdued concept involving Hong Kong Phooey. After hearing him out, DC's co-publisher told Hill, "I can see that you have a story you're a little scared of telling me about. But I want you to tell me that story. I can smell it on you. Give me that story." And it worked.

Very few people enjoy immediate success as writers. For most of us, it's a matter of staying in the game, continually focusing on refining our craft, diverting as much of our energy as possible into becoming the best writer we can be so that when an opportunity like that comes along, we're prepared to take it. Bryan Edward Hill got a shot to tell a story that he had nurtured for years—and the end result *was* as amazing as it had promised to be.

Chapter Five:

Finding Your Groove

A while back, hoping to improve my own writing practice, I read a book called *Atomic Habits*, which promised to reveal "an easy and proven way to build good habits and break bad ones." James Clear's advice is fairly solid as this genre goes; it's based (at least as I'm understanding it) in principles of behavioral psychology, and this cycle in particular:

cue ———→ craving ———→ response ———→ reward

Here's an example of this cycle from my own life: In the last apartment we lived in, I almost always reacted to the cue of going out by worrying about whether I'd locked the door, so I'd either turn the key a couple extra times or I'd get halfway down the stairs from the second floor to the lobby and then turn around and double-check the door again. It was never *not* locked, but the negative consequences that my response generated—extra time spent at the door, my wife's occasional exasperation— weren't so awful as to compel me to abandon the habit. So the craving for certainty didn't go away, and the peace of mind I got as a reward was worth it. (I did finally break the cycle, though—by moving to a new apartment.)

I've been thinking about this as it applies to cultivating a writing practice, and the cue part seems easy enough. You put your kids to bed; you sit down at your kitchen table; you open your notebook; you've got a solid hour before you need to turn in. Or your cue might be entirely different. It's whatever it is in your life that creates a situation that tells your mind, "Hey, this is a good time to do some writing!"

It's the next part that gets tricky. What is the *craving* that writing fulfills? Why would you initiate a writing practice? Some answers come to mind; a few chapters back, I mentioned "I want to be a bestselling author," or, rather, its two offshoots, "I want to make a lot of money" and "I want to be famous/recognized." But an actual writing practice doesn't satisfy those cravings, at least not in the way double-checking the front lock made me feel safer. You don't finish an hour of writing practice as a best-selling author unless you started it that way—and you already know what I think about writing with the intention of becoming a rich and/or famous writer.

So if wealth and fame aren't the rewards that make each round of writing satisfying enough for us to build up a habit that becomes a practice, what are those rewards? And what craving do they satisfy?

Another point Clear makes in *Atomic Habits* is that our habits are an expression of our idealized identity—who we want to be. You check your emails first thing every day when you get into the office because you want to be calm; I spent all that time checking the lock on my front door because I wanted to feel secure. If you see those examples as slightly negative—which they could be, if they interfered with our quality of life—let's pick examples that are unambiguously about enhancing our lives. I pour myself a glass of apple juice in the morning because I want to be healthy. You learn to fold your partner's laundry the way they like it, instead of the way your parents taught you, because you want to create a happy home environment.

If we frame writing as the means by which you transform yourself into the person you're "meant" to become, of sorting out the things that matter the most to you and assigning them actual priority in your life, then we could say that the *craving* writing satisfies is: "I want to know who I am."

Look at what you're writing. Are you writing about yourself? Okay, this just got a bit easier: What parts of your life are you choosing to write about? What are the patterns and themes that emerge from that writing . . . and what's your reaction to those themes? What self-images are falling away the more you reexamine your experiences, and what self-images are coming into shape?

If you're writing fiction, or narrative nonfiction, start by asking yourself, "What are the stories I'm choosing to tell?" You'll come up against many of the same questions I put to the memoirists. Why are these the themes that fascinate you? What do they tell you about the life you want to live and the world you want to live in? How has your understanding of yourself and your place in the world changed since you started trying to tell these stories?

The *reward* we get from each round of writing isn't instant nirvana, any more than it was wealth or fame. Ask any writer you know, and we'll gladly tell you that we aren't perfectly enlightened beings. (And if you meet one who says they *are* perfectly enlightened, start looking for the exits.) But just like every glass of apple juice reaffirms my efforts to live a healthy lifestyle, or every neatly folded pair of jeans expresses your commitment to a loving relationship, every writing session brings you . . .

. . . You know what? Now that I'm looking at it, I *don't* want to say *every* writing session brings you one step closer to enlightenment, because that implies there's an end point where enlightenment can absolutely for sure be achieved. Perhaps it's better to say writing will, on the best days, help you understand yourself a little better—and if it does lead to a breakthrough realization at some point, or various epiphanies at various points, that's awesome, but you should always be mindful of the small victories that accumulate along the way because they build one upon the other, ideally leading you to a creative and emotionally fulfilling life.

That's not just hype. Listen: You're a smart, creative person, and, deep down, you know what your imagination needs in order to flourish. You need to commit yourself to creating a life that enables you to surround yourself with that nourishment—but, also, don't simply *surround* yourself with it, *feed* yourself. All the inspirational books, all the supportive relationships . . . none of that will do you any good if you keep all your potential bottled up.

———————

Success will, in all likelihood, not come easily. But the way to become a writer who's capable of sharing her most powerful stories with the world is to give voice to your passions with every opportunity you can seize until that kind of self-awareness, authenticity, and clarity is simply the way you live your life.

I once saw a story on Buzzfeed about a woman who wrote her novel at a local tire shop. Amy Dawes had brought her car in to get the tires replaced and ended up having a creative outburst while she waited in the customer lounge. She wanted to repeat the experience, so she brought her friends' cars to the shop, hung out in the customer lounge while the mechanics changed the oil, and made headway on her manuscript each time. Eventually, she ran out of friends with cars she could borrow, at which point she asked the staff if she could just hang out and work on her book. They said sure, so that's what she did.

Sometimes I think about that story in terms of how we need to surround ourselves with people who "get" how important our writing is to us. Most of the time, it's your family and friends who are most likely to make accommodations that help you to do the writing you need to do. Or, because they know that this is something that matters to you, they'll give you a broader form of emotional support and encouragement, even as they acknowledge that you've given yourself a difficult challenge. (There's a world of difference between recognizing that something is hard and claiming that it's impossible or, more specifically, that it's probably impossible *for you*.)

The crew at Tires Tires Tires, though, went all in for someone who was practically a stranger. I mean, Amy Dawes had been in the shop often enough that they knew who she was by the time she asked whether she could stick around, but was still a customer rather than a close friend. That didn't matter to them. They not only invited her to write her book in the shop, they celebrated her presence . . . and her accomplishments!

Sometimes, though, I think about this story in terms of how we all try to find time and space in our busy days to write. We might be getting up an hour early, or taking a journal with us on the subway or on our lunch break, or cracking open the laptop while we're waiting for our kids to come out of school. For Amy Dawes, it was the customer lounge at an auto care center.

And that's great! But, when I talk to writers about the grunt work of writing, I always tell them not to fall into the trap of feeling like you can *only* work when everything is lined up just so. (I'm also the writer who once went to four separate office supply shops to find the particular type of blue pen that felt right in my hand so I could keep up my journal after the pen I was using dried up. We are none of us perfect.)

When I saw everyone getting excited by a story about a woman who found a place where she could start making some real creative headway, my mind went to the hypothetical moment when, say, the tire shop would have to close for renovations, or a new manager who wasn't as friendly took over. What would Amy do then? (I'm dark like that.)

When you hit upon a situation that can help make you a more productive writer, make the most of it! But don't, as my Quaker friends might say, mistake the form of the experience for its substance and start thinking that *this*, whatever *this* is, is what it takes to connect with your creativity. Use all the tools you can, but carry them lightly so you can put them down (if you ever need to) and still be able to continue working.

Now let me tell you what happened shortly after I originally wrote a version of the passage above for my newsletter.

I had been seeing a therapist once a week since 2004. We had moved the appointment around a couple times, when my work schedule or his required it, but apart from vacations, it had been a cornerstone of my week, a place I could go and talk about whatever was on my mind for forty-five minutes. Getting married, getting my first book published, getting a job, getting restructured *out* of that job five months later, getting another job, getting emotionally hammered by *that* job . . . Mark would hear me out, ask me follow-up questions, and nudge me in a direction where I could fix things for myself.

So, one Tuesday afternoon, we talked about the creative work I was doing at the time and what I could do to keep the momentum going. At the end of the session, I reminded him that I'd be out of town the following week, but we were still on for the week after that. He told me to have a good time while I was away and said he'd see me then.

Two weeks later, I showed up five minutes before my appointment and buzzed to be let into the reception lounge, but there was no response. That would happen sometimes, so I waited a few minutes and buzzed again. Still no response. Five minutes *after* our scheduled start, I texted him a friendly "We're still on today, right?" By now, somebody else had been able to get *his* therapist to buzz him in, so at least I was sitting down in the lounge. There was no response to the text, so I tried calling his cell phone, but the voice mail was full. Next I tried his landline, for the first time in at least a decade, but it had been disconnected.

And, you know, the penny probably should have dropped then, but honestly I figured, well, yeah, who bothers with a landline these days if they can help it? When I talked about Mark's no-show with my wife that evening, we both expressed hope that everything was okay, but my initial reaction was either that he'd simply gotten it into his head that I'd be gone for two weeks or, more likely, something had come up at home that he'd had to deal with and he'd be apologetic the following week and everything would carry on as before.

Except that he never answered my text, and he didn't answer my (slightly more concerned) email the next day, or the follow-up email I sent after the weekend had passed with no response, or the text explaining that I'd like to hear back from him before I came into Manhattan again for our next scheduled appointment. By now, I'd run a search in Google News to see if I could find out whether anything had happened to him, but nothing came up. Finally, a few hours before my appointment, I was on the phone with my wife, wondering if I should even go into the city since I still hadn't heard from him, and *she* had the objectivity to look him up on Legacy.com, where we learned that he'd died while we were out of town.

Fortunately, as a sympathetic friend said when I told her all this, "After fourteen years in therapy, you've probably got the major issues sorted out, and were just working on routine maintenance." And it's true: I was in a position where I didn't feel like I was at any immediate emotional risk, so I could explore my options calmly and carefully. Not everybody gets that, and I realize how lucky I was that I did.

Now, let's change this from a story about me to a lesson about our writing practices. It's important to have people around us who are truly supportive of our writing, and if we're fortunate enough to segue from writing for ourselves to working with the publishing industry, it's also important to align ourselves with supportive professionals—not people who will do whatever we want, of course, but people who will help us recognize what's best for our writing, even if we don't see it ourselves at first, and will work with us to achieve that. Literary agents, for example, or editors, or publicists, among others.

Even when we're lucky enough to find them, though, people like that won't be with us forever. Literary agents retire. Editors sign up your book for their publishing house and then they take a job somewhere else and you're reassigned to somebody who isn't nearly as familiar with your work. Heck, I know authors who've had four different publicists assigned to their book from the day that the publisher acquired it to the day it hit bookstores. (Usually, it's more like two, *maybe* three, but this publishing company had particularly high turnover.)

These things sting when they happen, but you can't take them personally, and you can't let them knock you off your game. Just do your best to keep moving forward and hope that the people with whom you'll be working next can be as helpful (or more so!) than the ones who came before them. And remember that even when people are no longer in a position to help you *directly*, they can still be informal advocates for you and your work. You might have an editor who's so enthusiastic about your writing that she recommends your books to friends long after you've stopped working together, or a publicist who assures her successor that you're a pleasure to work with, or . . . The point is: even in setbacks, positive possibilities exist.

Cherish the relationships that you form over the course of your writing career, and be mindful of how they've helped you advance toward becoming the writer you want to be. At the same time, though, remember that they didn't *make* you that writer. You did that, by putting in the work, and if you should find yourself in a position where their help is no longer available to you, you'll have to find a way to keep doing that work without them once you've finished mourning the loss—or, to be fully honest about it, *as* you're mourning the loss.

I can tell you from experience, it's not like you'll just wake up one morning and get back to work as if nothing had happened. Of course not. You just have to be able to get back to work as if all this has happened and you're dealing with it the best you can, by being the writer your agent, your editor, your publicist, your partner, your friends, or your therapist have helped you become.

———

Sometimes, though, no matter how much support you get from those around you, the words don't come out right. If that goes on long enough, you might start to worry that they'll never come out right—or, worse yet, that you're incapable of finding the right words, that you're a failure as a writer, and that your friends are either indulging you or just haven't figured out yet that you're a fraud. But they will, you'll tell yourself, they will . . .

I should confess, because it may affect how you perceive the advice that follows, that I've never suffered from the form of imposter syndrome I've just described. I'm not saying I never doubt my work, because I doubt my work on a regular basis—but I don't think I'm a fraud, and I'm not worried you'll figure out I'm a fraud some day. I'm actually rather confident of my talent and my abilities; what gets inside my head is the fear that I'm not writing up to my potential, that I could do much better, and I'm settling for less out of . . . I don't know, exhaustion, or laziness, or cowardice, or *something*.

But then I turn the essay in, and the feedback is encouraging, and, well, I trust my editors and my readers know what they're talking about, and that if I *did* suck, they'd let me know. So, over time, I've gotten better at pushing the doubt away and choosing to believe that I'm handing in good work—especially in those cases where I'm working with an editor who *will* push me to fix the parts that aren't as effective as they can be—and I don't necessarily need to be perfect at the start.

This may feel like a digression, but bear with me: When I was twenty-eight, I was hired by Amazon to serve as a "nonfiction editor," which—although it came with a great deal of license—boiled down to writing and editing marketing copy for fifty to sixty books a month. With two decades of hindsight, I'd approach the editing side of that job differently now, but I got to be pretty good at the writing side.

Gradually, though, I came to feel that, while this was a fantastic opportunity, the task of book reviewing was not an inherently remarkable one. I was very good at it, yes, but it was something any number of people could do just as well, if not better. The difference was that I had chosen to spend my teens reading everything I could get my hands on, then spent my twenties developing my critical skills as an undergraduate, a grad student, and a freelance reviewer— while continuing to read as widely and as deeply as the time available to me allowed.

I never doubted that I was *good* at what I did; I just didn't think I was *special*. Years later, I read an essay by a literary critic who claimed that "criticism is a genre that one has to have a knack for," one for which, he believed, "very few people are suited." I disagree; I think we all have the potential to become critics, just as we all have the potential to become novelists or poets. We don't *have* the qualities that make us good in those fields, we *cultivate* them, because we *choose* to do so. (For some of us, circumstance makes that choice easier than it is for others.)

I still believe that holds true not just for literary criticism, but for any other form of creative writing (or any other artistic pursuit for that matter). I've put in enough time and effort— the 10,000 hours, as Malcolm Gladwell might put it—to develop a fair amount of writing skills, but I know I'm far from the best at what I do, and at a certain point, I stopped worrying about being "the best" in comparison to any other writers out there. Now I just worry about being "the best I can be." That's an ongoing project with no end in sight—and, as long as what I write continues to reflect my deepest concerns, how can I be an impostor?

Video essayist Lindsay Ellis made me rethink my opinion of impostor syndrome, though, when she shared her thoughts on the subject on Twitter. The model she laid out wasn't just about feeling like a fraud; it also included feeling like you're not good enough—a feeling that can be exacerbated by trying to write in the face of unrelenting criticism. If people tell you often enough that your work isn't good enough, you might just start to believe it. And if you've never had to deal with that, Ellis says, you don't *know* how to deal with it.

"Dismissing negative thoughts isn't helpful for the people who have them," she explained. "It is a form of invalidating emotions, and the root of these negative thoughts isn't logic, but self-image."

That sounded like it was at odds with my own belief that I've never dealt with impostor syndrome, and Ellis went on to describe a mental process that seemed similar to what I just wrote about my recurring doubts:

Every time I hit a milestone, I don't feel secure in it—
I've already moved the goal post before I even realize
I've succeeded at [Thing]. But the goal post has been
moved, therefore the thing is not a success.

I think Ellis offers a truly valuable distinction between
perfectionism, which can be used "to create better, more
thoughtful work," and catastrophizing, or allowing negative
thoughts to put you into a tailspin. You might recognize your
own writing experience at one pole or the other, or fluctuating
wildly between both.

That's not exactly how I feel, though—by the time I hit
the milestone, my insecurities *have* usually been addressed,
mostly because I don't move my internal goalposts.

Let me give you a specific example: I once spent an entire
evening trying to figure out how I could cut 665 words down
to 600 for a freelance newspaper assignment, because print
outlets are actually serious about their word counts and space
constraints. In the end, all I could think to do was to highlight
approximately forty-five words and tell my editor, "These
sentences look like you could probably cut them if you have
to. After that, I'm open to suggestion."

The answer turned out to be, well, the first three
paragraphs are okay, but I had taken a wrong turn after that,
so could I write less about *those* things and more about *these*
things? Which, to be fair, isn't unusual when you start writing
a story with a very broad idea about the subject matter and
you figure out your angles as you go along, then you give it
to the editor and she realizes she has all sorts of questions
about things you didn't bring up. My editor also provided
a link to an example of the kind of story she had in mind,

which gave me a clearer roadmap for writing the second draft of the article.

So I spent the next afternoon stripping out a lot of the boring details, leaving a few behind because they still felt essential to the story or at least interesting enough to retain. I jumped back into the book to find similar elements to add to the feature, and when I came up for air, I realized I now had 700 words. Well, that wouldn't do, so I emailed my editor and admitted I was running long, but if I was moving in the right direction, I could spend some time later in the evening figuring out how to lose 100 words without disrupting the narrative flow.

Except I still hadn't answered enough of the *real* questions she had. I was, essentially, trying to save my original concept by hanging new ornaments off its branches, and my editor was saying, no, it was time to go back into the woods and find another tree. Luckily, she was willing to give me the time to do that, and the article that I eventually turned in was better for the additional work that went into it.

This is what I do with my developmental editing clients all the time. They show me stories that are generally *okay*: the copy's pretty clean, the stories have beginnings, middles, and ends, and so on. I read the manuscripts, and then I write the authors back. This part's confusing, I might say. Why is this character suddenly behaving this way? I understand why this *needs* to happen, but is there another, more natural-feeling way it could happen? What if you looked at this sequence of events from *her* point of view instead of *his*?

I hope I get it right with my clients. I know from experience, when I'm on the receiving end, at least with the editors I've been fortunate enough to work with, all the questions and the prompts really *do* push me in a better direction and lead me to more dynamic stories. A good writer can probably find that path on her own, eventually, but sometimes it's good to have a guide to help you get there sooner.

Chapter Six:

Your Voice Is Valuable

I once semi-jokingly said on Twitter that I wanted to be Anthony Bourdain when I grew up.

At the time, Bourdain had only recently moved to CNN and was still fine-tuning the ways in which his show there, *Parts Unknown,* would distinguish itself from his Travel Channel program, *No Reservations.* By then, though, as a viewer, it seemed to me that the basic principles of Bourdain's project had been locked into place—in each episode, he used local food as a starting point to tell stories about other people, their lives, their traditions, and the challenges they faced.

The reason I wanted to be like Bourdain is that I thought he had achieved an ideal vocation: somehow, he had gotten other people to pay for him to travel the world and spend time learning about the things that fascinated him the most, then share what he had learned with his audience. At an abstract level, that's a perfect setup for a writer. Maybe we don't all dream of becoming world travelers, but I think most of us would welcome the possibility of being able to devote ourselves to the stories that compel us, as opposed to carving out whatever time we could for those stories around all the other responsibilities in our lives.

Just as importantly, as far as those of us watching at home could tell, success hadn't warped Bourdain's character. It would be foolish to pretend that a large influx of money, especially one that turns into a steady stream, isn't going to change a person's life. But while success and fame opened up a rich matrix of possibilities, it didn't seem to cut Bourdain off from who he had been before that success. He felt as authentic on television as he had in the pages of *Kitchen Confidential* nearly two decades earlier.

I thought Anthony Bourdain was living the dream—but we know now that, no matter how much he may have been able to take pleasure in the life he'd created for himself, there was another current running through that life. It was one he pushed against for years, and, for whatever reason, one night in France, his resistance finally gave out.

It occurred to me the morning I learned of his death that we all know somebody who's dealing with depression or anxiety—and if we don't, it might be because we aren't looking closely enough. There's one thing, then, blatantly obvious though it may be: Pay more attention to the people around you. Another observation a number of people shared on social media as the news spread feels just as important: There's no "one-size-fits-all" solution; what helps one person might be counterproductive for another. Don't charge into someone's life thinking that you're going to "make things right." Be present, be responsive, but don't act like you have all the answers.

As we learned in discussing imposter syndrome, if you're a writer, a creative person of any kind really, you're probably familiar, to some degree, with feelings of inadequacy and failure, even if you've never been diagnosed with depression or anxiety. I'll be the first to tell you that as much as I have accomplished as a writer and an editor, I've never fully shaken off all the things I *haven't* accomplished—failed attempts, outright rejections, and unstarted ideas galore. One of the most useful tools therapy gave me, after all the years I spent with Mark, is the ability to recognize the doubts and insecurities surrounding what I haven't done with my life *as* doubts and insecurities, not as external judgments. But they still come up; I still face them.

If you're going through something similar right now, as you're reading this book, please know that what you're experiencing is normal. One metaphor I find helpful is that when you decide to be a writer, you set out on a path. You may not make it as far down that path as you would like, or as quickly as you would like, but that doesn't make you a failure. And when you start to feel like a failure, it might be helpful to remember why you set out on this path in the first place: What's the thing that *you* found so compelling you needed to share it with the rest of the world? If you've lost touch with it, what can you do to renew the connection? Or, if you can't figure out how to get it out in front of the world, what can you do differently?

———

When you get lost on that path, though, it can take a long time to find your way back, as I learned when I read Deborah Levy's *Things I Don't Want to Know*. At first, the slim memoir didn't feel like it was living up to the promises of its subtitle: *On Writing*. Instead, it careened from a recent existential crisis to Levy's childhood in apartheid-era South Africa to adolescent exile in England and finally back to the near-present. A writer's block of some kind appeared to be at the heart of the crisis, but the book wasn't about writer's block, not directly.

There's a line close to the end of the book, though, where, for me at least, things finally fell into place, as Levy realizes that she's been struggling to ask herself two very specific questions: "What do we do with knowledge that we cannot bear to live with? What do we do with the things we do not want to know?"

Then Levy remembers something else she'd realized recently: "To become a writer, I had to learn to interrupt, to speak up, to speak a little louder, and then louder, and then to just speak in my own voice which is not loud at all." It's an insight that she connects back to her childhood experiences, but also to her occasional citation of feminist writers like Julia Kristeva, Marguerite Duras, and Virginia Woolf.

That theme—the circumstances of the woman writer—returns forcefully in Levy's follow-up book, *The Cost of Living*, billed as "a working autobiography." In it, Levy talks explicitly about the aftershocks of her divorce and her subsequent efforts to find the room to write while rebuilding her life . . . by which she means not just the time and space and emotional energy, but (having moved with her daughter into a cramped apartment) an actual room.

Writing, Levy reminds us, can't be separated from our necessary existence in the material world. Or, for that matter, the cultural world imposed on the material world—and here Levy has some very pointed observations about, for example, the apparent inability of some men to remember the name of "my wife" when talking about her to other people.

Unless you are very fortunate, when you choose to become a writer, you are choosing to take on a pursuit that reality, at multiple levels, will discourage both actively and passively. Figuring out what you're compelled to share with the world, and then honing your voice to share that story, is not an easy process; even if you can carve out time around your various obligations, even if you can block out the admonitions and warnings of the people around you, chances are you will arrive at a moment when you ask yourself: "What the hell am I doing here?"

You'll almost certainly have moments like that at the beginning of your writing life, when you're first struggling to define your "mission." You might have an idea for a story, but it's still somewhat amorphous, and you're not quite sure how you can transform it from an idea to a story, or if you even have what it takes to do that. So you start doing the work, and you find out whether or not you have what it takes.

But, as Levy's two books reveal, early success is no guarantee that you won't face that dilemma again. Perhaps you'll find yourself at a creative dead end. Or life might throw you a curveball, leaving you unsure about whether you can continue writing. Whatever the reason, you'll need to ground yourself, reassert your commitment. I'm not saying you should bury yourself in "writing" in order to avoid problems going on in other corners of your life. In fact, I tend to think the opposite is true—that we need to organize the rest of our lives as smoothly *as possible* in order to create a reliable "space" for our writing.

"At this uncertain time," Levy writes of her postdivorce life, "writing was one of the few activities in which I could handle the anxiety of uncertainty, of not knowing what was going to happen next." When the rest of our lives are secure, whether it's because we've set up a steady job for ourselves or we have a supportive partner or however we've made it happen, we can *lean into* the insecurity of writing and find our story, and ourselves, as we go along.

Most of us, though, aren't likely to have a completely secure life; something's always going to come up. So the question is whether we can learn to lean into the uncertainty of writing, of daring to make what might be a false start, of hitting upon a late discovery that forces us to rethink everything that's come before, while all that other uncertainty is swirling around us.

Here's another story along those lines: I interviewed Dani Shapiro after one of her memoirs, *Inheritance*, came out. She'd written about inadvertently learning, thanks to a commercial DNA test, that her father wasn't her biological father, and grappling with the identity crises that rippled out from that discovery. As I was transcribing the audio file a few days after our phone call, I was struck by her response when I asked how she saw her writing moving forward. She told me *Inheritance* was probably the last narrative-driven project she saw herself writing, that she had become more interested, over the course of her last few books, in probing consciousness than telling a straightforward narrative—until she got that DNA test back, and was plunged into a *huge* story.

It was the part that came next that really resonated with me, though:

> As a writer, everything I've ever written about has led to this. If I look at the beginning of my writing life, my first novels and my earlier memoirs, I was always in some way or another, especially in my fiction, writing about family secrets. It was something that I returned to again and again as a fiction writer, and now I know why. The discovery is that I was the secret.

If we think about writing as a process of figuring out what matters most deeply to you and then learning how to share that with other people, a quest undertaken by both fiction writers and nonfiction writers, sometimes we discover, as Dani Shapiro did, that we can hit upon the stories that captivate us long before we realize *why* they captivate us.

Does self-awareness make for "better" stories? I've given that a lot of thought, and the best answer I've got, which might be either not all that helpful or exactly what you need to hear, is: Sometimes it does, sometimes it doesn't. Obviously, when you've got an author who understands why these things matter to her, and she's prepared to attempt to persuade you they matter, self-awareness can be a critical component in a story's success.

But I believe it's also possible to tell a compelling story that is intuitively important to you without fully recognizing why that story has a grip on you—and perhaps, in some ways, it could be a stronger story for running on unconscious drives, freeing you to depict a sequence of events or a state of being without feeling the urge to explain What It All Means.

As with so many aspects of the writing life, there's no one-size-fits-all answer, other than to try to do the most you're capable of doing at any given moment.

———————

As much as I love to hammer home the importance of loving what you do, and having the clarity of purpose that allows you to dedicate yourself to writing when it's generally a financially dubious venture, I want to be clear: It's important for you to respect your work, to know its value, and to decline to let other people take advantage of you.

Over the years, for example, I've encouraged people not to write for outlets, such as the *Huffington Post*, that take contributions from writers without paying for them, then generate revenue off publishing that material. Getting paid might not be the *primary* reason you choose to write a novel, or a work of narrative nonfiction, or an essay, or even a poem—especially a poem, ha ha—but it's always worth stopping to think before you give that work away to somebody else so *they* can profit from it without giving you a piece of the action. (And, no, I *don't* think "exposure" is sufficient compensation for the creative struggle.)

I was reminded of this a while back when fantasy and horror writer Seanan McGuire posted to Twitter, expressing her frustration at finding the text of her upcoming novel on an illegal download site more than a week before the book's scheduled release, something that would undoubtedly have a significant negative impact on the sales of that book.

McGuire talked openly about the emotional labor that went into the writing. "Does it help to know that I spent the better part of a year researching the folklore and mythology that underpins the story?" she asked. "Or that I cried at several points when writing, because I needed things to fit together JUST SO, and couldn't quite get there?"

"Until I transcend this crude flesh and become a being of moonlight and shadow, art has to be about money," she continued. "I have to be able to eat, and keep my lights on, and pay my vet bills, and pay my mortgage. If I'm too busy panicking about those things to think, I'm not making art. Fear and panic and pain are not the wellsprings of creativity."

Like it or not, in our capitalist system, one of the most effective ways to stave off fear and panic and pain is to purchase your (temporary) freedom from them, and that takes money, and if you can't make the money making your art, you've got to make it doing something else, which takes away time from doing your art.

Happily enough, in this case, the folks at Black Phoenix Alchemy Lab, a very hip perfume company, saw McGuire's tweets and actually reached out to her, declaring their interest in creating perfumes inspired by the book. It isn't a guaranteed happy ending for McGuire, but it's more of an opportunity than most writers in her situation get.

Soon after McGuire's public shaming of the people pirating her novel, the bookish corners of social media became fascinated by the story of Heather Demetrios, a novelist who received huge advances from major publishers for her earliest books, only to see those books perform below expectations, as a result of which her advances got smaller and smaller. The essay she wrote about all this, which she posted online, had a distinct undercurrent of "Why didn't anybody tell me this could happen?"

Actually, it wasn't an undercurrent at all. It was right out there for everyone to see, from the second sentence onward, frequently in bold type. Despite two separate six-figure book deals, Demetrios wrote, she "somehow missed several critical aspects of the business," adding: "That was on me, to some extent."

No, I would counter, that was *entirely* on her.

Some context: Years before I became an acquisitions editor, I was a freelance writer who met an editor at a now-defunct imprint of a large publishing conglomerate, found out we both loved 1970s films, and turned that shared interest into a book proposal, which led to a modest but respectable contract offer, which I then used to convince an agent to represent me. I told my agent I was prepared to accept the offer because of the way the book deal had come together, but I wanted to know if there were any details in the contract she'd suggest should be negotiated—and when she found some, I paid attention to her advice. At the time, I was also covering the publishing industry as a (full-time freelance) day job, so in that sense, I was paying more-than-typical attention to how things work in this industry, but we weren't exactly dealing in state secrets here.

So, by the time I took that editorial job with a publishing company and started sending out boilerplate contracts to authors (through their literary agents), I happened to know there were clauses in those contracts that *I* would never accept if they were handed to me—and that a good agent, mindful of her author's career, would reject those clauses as well.

Now, would I *say* that to an agent? Not if I had wanted to keep my job. As much as an editor might sympathize with their authors and want them to succeed, their ultimate role in the book deal is to represent the publishing house's interests, to keep the house from throwing away too much money on failed projects.

Notice I said *too much* money. Because it's one of the not-so-secret secrets of the industry that book publishers throw money away on books *all the time*. Not deliberately, of course; it's just that no matter how great someone's "intuition" or "sense of the market" might be, it's largely a gamble—and, from the house's perspective, especially at the Big 5/New York level, they "overpay" for many, if not most, of their acquisitions, the main question being whether they overpaid by a little or by a lot.

Notice, too, that I said *failed* projects, and not "bad books." Except in very rare cases that usually involve celebrities from non-literary fields, nobody in publishing wants to gamble on a *bad* book. Before offering an author an advance, editors have to make intense calculations as to how well they believe a book can sell and how much it will cost to produce a book that sells that many copies. The size of the advance gets factored into that analysis; how much money can the house give up and still turn a profit if the book meets that benchmark?

To put it simply: Publishing houses do not exist to make authors money . . . save to the extent that, in doing so, *they make money for themselves as well.*

If you're familiar with the investment world, think about a book publisher as a venture capital firm. An author comes to them with what is essentially a business plan: *This is a book that people will pay money to own and to read, and I'm the person who can make it good enough for them to do that.* If the publisher agrees, it will commit material resources to the production and distribution of that book in exchange for a substantial cut of the revenue.

When the investment pays off, everybody's happy. When there's some success, but not quite enough to earn the investor dividends, sometimes the relationship between the entrepreneur and the investor (the author and the publisher) is strong enough that the investor is still willing to see if the entrepreneur's next idea will click with the market—although they might be understandably cautious about how much money they would sink into that next project.

And sometimes, when a project flops, for whatever reason, the investor will just never go back to that particular well again. In a worst-case scenario, it might be because the author and the publisher wound up at each other's throats, but it's far more likely that the publisher simply gets skittish—and, if we're being fully honest, manages to convince itself that the problem was with the book, rather than with its own "sense of the market" or the way it handled the good thing it had. In any event, the investor just can't work up the nerve to keep funneling money to that entrepreneur, leaving the entrepreneur to find someone else willing to take a chance.

So, as an author, if you're facing the happy prospect of publication, you need to know that the publishing house is not eager to work with you out of pure artistic spirit. I don't just mean you need to grasp that intellectually; I mean you need to know, deep down in your gut, that the publishing house sees in you an opportunity to make money, and that as much as the people working there might, in an ideal situation, like you personally and hope for your success, at the end of the day, your usefulness to them depends on your ability to reward their investment, and that your relationship very likely has an end date on it, even if neither of you knows when that might be.

If you want to prolong that relationship, you need to apply yourself to the following question: "What can I do to make my investors money?" And as much as you would like the answer to be "keep writing books for them," your publisher generally won't see it that way unless the existing books are *already* making money.

So what's the answer, then? It pretty much boils down to marketing. You chose to become a writer because you had something you wanted to share with the world. You worked on your craft to improve your ability to share your story (or message, or vision), but that ability isn't limited to your craft.

What can you do to make as much of your life as possible, not just your writing practice, a vehicle for your story?

———————

Ultimately, though, Heather Demetrios wasn't telling a story about the publishing industry, or even about being a writer—her story was about being inadequately prepared to handle financial success, period, and that's another story I know something about.

I didn't get a six-figure book advance when I was in my twenties, but I was lucky enough to land that job at Amazon I told you about earlier, back when it was still only selling books, and was officially there exactly two years—which means that I had two anniversaries where I could buy significant chunks of Amazon stock.

The first year, I was actually smart about things, and I paid off the balance on my student loans and my credit card, parking the rest in a mutual fund. A year later, though, although I did put a little more into the mutual fund, I decided I was done with Seattle and I was ready to try my luck in New York City. Not to become a full-time writer—I wasn't that ambitious—but I figured I would have a bit of a safety net while I looked for my next job in the book world.

So my rent doubled, and drinks got a lot more expensive. I was thirty years old and single, and long story short, although I did have a six-month period of gainful employment during which I learned I was not cut out to be a publicist, the money lasted a little under two years.

As things got tighter, though, I *didn't* ask myself why nobody had warned me this could have happened, because I could recognize exactly what mistakes I'd made, and they were my own fault—but also a lot of personally rewarding things came out of that period, including the relationship that led to my marriage, so I refused to beat myself up emotionally about all that too much or to indulge in *Sliding Doors*-type woolgathering.

People often come into success woefully unprepared for how it might change their lives, and the fact that this happened to Heather Demetrios with a book advance, or to me with vested stock options, is in many ways incidental to the theme and not a reflection on the book publishing industry or the dot-com industry or whatever.

It probably says something, though, about how certain segments of a particularly American capitalist society were taught to view money and success in the latter half of the twentieth century, and about a persistent strain in our cultural imagination that emphasizes the *creative* aspects of being a published author and often refuses to acknowledge the *commercial* and *economic* aspects of that vocation.

The musician and meditation teacher David Nichtern seemed like he would be tackling that subject in his book, *Creativity, Spirituality, and Making a Buck*, which I picked up soon after the Heather Demetrios story made its splash. Nichtern certainly talked the right talk, with a declaration for all creative types that is relevant to our writing practices: "We're really trying to balance aspiration, ambition, effort, and accomplishment with a sense of reasonableness, ease, and satisfaction."

He comes from a Buddhist background, so there's a lot of emphasis in the book on mindfulness—in particular, on developing one's clarity, intention, and focus in order to better understand what it is you're meant to be doing and, from there, to get it done. If you're completely new to Buddhism, you're not going to get lost, and if you do know what Nichtern's talking about, it's all pretty straightforward.

At one point, he introduces readers to "poverty mentality," a concept similar to "impostor syndrome" that he borrows from his mentor, Chigyam Trungpa Rinpoche. "Instead of coming from a place of inherent richness and courage," Nichtern writes, "we lead with a feeling that failure is inevitable. And then, of course, our projection becomes a self-fulfilling prophecy."

I imagine you can pick out a moment in your past when your writing has fallen prey to some form of this kind of thinking. Maybe it's something you stopped writing because you didn't think you could figure out how to finish it. Maybe it's something you never even started to write because you were afraid you couldn't do the topic justice or you were afraid of what other people might say about it.

A story you never submitted because you "knew" it would be rejected. An application to a workshop or an MFA program you never completed because you "knew" you'd just be wasting your time.

To be clear, though, none of this is about actual, material poverty, the kind of poverty that keeps you from sending in your stories because you can't afford the submission fees, that keeps you from applying to creative writing programs because you can't afford the tuition, that keeps you from writing because at the end of a full working day, you're physically and emotionally exhausted. Instead, as Nichtern explains, it's about the ways in which even people with plenty of opportunities in life can still manage to sell themselves short:

> What's missing . . . is kindness and compassion toward ourselves. If we have deeply embedded habits of being too harsh and unfriendly toward ourselves, it can be very challenging to practice mindfulness.

It's the same with writing. You need to believe, deep down, that you can do it, then you need to give yourself permission to do it—and that involves clearing space and time in your life to devote to your writing practice, because it *is* a thing that matters. You have to be willing to forgive yourself your initial missteps, to push past them and keep moving forward, because it *matters* that you keep moving forward.

(I say "initial missteps," but the truth is you're going to keep making them no matter how long you stick with the program, so you might as well get used to forgiving yourself early.)

I also noticed that Nichtern kept coming back, over and over, to the concept of your creative output as an "offering," something that made immediate sense to me. Once you realize that you *can* act from a position of abundance, that you *can* make a valuable contribution, it's easier to say, "This is what I have to give."

Of course, thinking about our writing as an offering, or a gift, just brings us back to the fundamental problem. The point of a gift is that you don't expect to receive anything in return—but, the capitalist system being what it is, if you want to dedicate more than a fraction of your life to your writing practice, you're eventually going to *need* something in return, and how are you supposed to go about getting it?

On that front, I wish *Creativity, Spirituality, and Making a Buck* had been a bit stronger, as Nichtern's advice never seemed to get very far past cultivating a basic awareness of the realities of the commercial world. I felt that it was talking *around* the subject well enough, but I wanted something I could clasp more firmly than, say, "know your market" or "master the elevator pitch."

(It didn't help that his examples of elevator pitches were pretty banal, like describing *Star Wars* as "a sci-fi, samurai-ish, good-versus-evil galactic space epic." Which is true, up to a point, but it isn't *compelling*. Pitching "a sci-fi, samurai-ish, good-versus-evil galactic space epic" to someone might get you a "huh" in response, but nobody's going to buy into it the way they might buy into, say, "An evil empire is poised to dominate the galaxy, but there's this kid on a backwater planet, and he's about to embark on a journey that will bring the whole thing tumbling down" might. That's a *story* that makes someone ask *who?* and *how?* and *why?* and not be content until they learn some answers. Or, at least, it's closer to that kind of story than "a galactic space epic.")

If the book wasn't particularly helpful in terms of navigating the "business" side of a creative vocation, though, I think the emphasis on mindfulness does offer useful insights into dealing with the "creative" side. Becoming more aware of how we can get in the way of our own development is one such insight. There's another moment where Nichtern talks about meditation and how, if we take it up seriously, "most of us will experience frustration, boredom, irritation, doubt, anxiety, and any and every other feeling we've had, were never comfortable with, and have been running away from for most of our lives."

That pretty much sums up every bad day you've had in the writing chair, right? I know it sums up plenty of mine. And the "solution" is the same as it is in the meditation world:

Acknowledge the difficulties and keep going.

And don't be afraid to ask for help! So many other writers are facing the same crises and can share their coping strategies or even just offer an empathetic ear. So many other people in your life are willing to be there for you—and if you don't feel comfortable talking to your family or friends, about exposing those raw nerves to somebody so close, there are professionals who can help you as well. Whatever option you choose, don't be afraid to seek out assistance when you need it, *as soon as you need it.*

Don't put off asking for help because you think you're not suffering enough for your pain to really matter, or because you think you should be able to tackle it on your own.

I realized, as I was writing the opening paragraph to this chapter, that when I said I wanted to be Anthony Bourdain when I grew up, I was roughly the same age he was when *Kitchen Confidential* came out, forty-three years old. He'd done a lot before then, certainly; in fact, he'd already published two novels in the years immediately preceding that book's publication—in addition to his legendary culinary career. But he was forty-three when his life kicked into a higher gear, and one of the things I'm choosing to take away from that is that we don't know when success might come for us, so don't ever tell yourself that it's too late. And, if it does come, treat it not as an opportunity to reward yourself gratuitously—instead, indulge yourself by pouring even more energy and attention into what made you a success so that you can share even more great stories with us.

Don't be surprised, though, if your success is accompanied by doubt and insecurity. Try to be prepared, try to have a support system in place, try to face your fears down as best you can—and remember you don't have to face them alone.

WHEN
YOU DECIDE TO BE
A WRITER, YOU SET OUT ON
A PATH. YOU MAY NOT MAKE IT
AS FAR DOWN THAT PATH AS YOU
WOULD LIKE, OR AS QUICKLY AS YOU
WOULD LIKE, BUT THAT DOESN'T
MAKE YOU A FAILURE.

Chapter Seven:

Pacing Yourself for the Long Haul

Yuou picked up this book because you wanted to "be a writer," and no matter how far along you are in that process, it's almost inevitable that you've been comparing yourself to another writer. Maybe it's one of the other members of your writing group, or some novelist who got profiled in a newspaper or a magazine, or a best-selling author you follow on Twitter who always manages to be dazzling, even when she's telling everyone how far behind she is on her copyedits.

Those kinds of comparisons tend to leave you on the losing end.

So stop making them.

There's a book that managed to sit on my bookshelf for more than half a decade before I finally picked it up, called *Running with the Mind of Meditation*. It's by Sakyong Mipham, who had been an acclaimed meditation teacher until—although I didn't realize this until I was well into the book—several credible accusations of sexual misconduct forced him to step down from that role. (He started teaching again in early 2020, which might go to show that Buddhist institutions are just as susceptible to patriarchy as any sector of Western society.)

Mipham was also a marathon runner, and his core argument was that the discipline of becoming a good runner is similar to the discipline of becoming a good meditator. He emphasized cultivating a self-awareness of your body in the same way you would cultivate a self-awareness of your mind, and this passage jumped out at me as particularly helpful:

> When ambition is our main motivation, it throws us out of balance. Running on self-worth completely eliminates the need to become overly arrogant and put others down when they aren't running on our level. We save energy that way. Self-worth even allows us to appreciate the talents of other athletes without feeling threatened by them.

Your writing practice isn't a competition. You're not working on your writing so you can craft better sentences and receive better reviews than Jane Doe, or get a better book deal than her, or sell more books than her—or, at least, you shouldn't be. You probably *could* do any or all of those things if you set your mind to it, but those aren't the markers of success you should be focused on.

You certainly shouldn't be working from a mindset in which your success is dependent on *outperforming* any other writer, as if there's a finite amount of success available in the literary world and you need to grab it before somebody else does. Publishing is not a zero-sum game. There's room for plenty of people to succeed, and while there will obviously be quantitative differences between one writer's success and another's, you don't need to fixate on them. You can be confident in what you've accomplished and have mental and emotional space left over to acknowledge, even admire, the accomplishments of others.

And "what you've accomplished" is, of course, more than just getting good reviews, or scoring a huge advance, or landing on a bestseller list, if you're fortunate enough to have those things happen. The success you really ought to focus on isn't that success of ambition but the success of self-worth. It comes when you recognize that, through your writing practice, you've not only discovered something that means a lot to you that you want to share with the world, you've discovered *how* to share it in a meaningful way. You've realized something powerful within yourself—*about yourself*, even—and you've given it expression.

Don't get me wrong: It's fantastic to be able to do that *and* get thousands and thousands of people to buy into it. And though it's possible to get thousands and thousands of people to buy something totally market-driven that doesn't actually come from the heart, too, I can't imagine that it feels all *that* great, even as the royalties pour in. When you're constantly writing to the market, you have to continually second-guess yourself, wondering if you're falling out of step with what's hot. When you focus on listening to the still, small voice within yourself, you can always count on the results connecting with *someone*, somewhere down the line.

Let's stay with the metaphor of running, because I want to share a story I read in a newsletter written by Terrell Johnson called *The Half Marathoner*, about how Roger Bannister broke the four-minute mile in 1954.

I'd never realized that Bannister was an amateur runner and had been competing in races around his schedule as a medical student. Because of that, his training regimen wasn't all that extensive—as he once put it, "I trained for less than three-quarters of an hour, maybe five days a week—*I didn't have time to do more.*"

The first time I read that story, my mind kept circling back to the fact that Bannister didn't run a mile in three minutes, fifty-nine seconds because he had dedicated his entire life to that purpose, but that he had found time to become a person capable of running at that speed around everything else he had going on in his life at the time.

You can probably see where I'm going with this, because you've tried to figure out where in your packed schedule you have time to write. The good news is that you don't have to drop *everything* else in your life in order to tell a great story. You just have to make telling that story a priority in your life and carve some time out of each day (or as near to each day as possible) to honor that priority.

Roger Bannister was able to fit his running practice into a little under four hours a week, and it took him just about two years to reach his goal. What could *you* accomplish in four hours a week if you gave your best to crafting a story in those bursts of time? What might you have to show for it in two years?

If that possibility excites you, here's another question, from a different *Half Marathoner* essay, this one by Carissa Liebowitz: "If left to our own devices with free time and adequate resources, what would we choose to do?"

If Liebowitz had been writing about writing, she might have continued: *It's a reasonably safe bet that nobody's going to give you that time or those resources but yourself. Sure, there are residencies and workshops and such, but even those are things you'll need to apply for. So, one way or another, get to it.*

Her essay, however, is about a expedition she took with a small group on their way to a marathon, and she recounts how, after several days together, they began to tell each other about intimate moments in their lives, including what she describes as "darker secrets." As she writes, "The higher the level of suffering, the more it seems we are willing to open up and offer the true versions of ourselves":

> I've found that I'm the most authentic version of myself in the midst of a long training run or deep into a tough race. The things I might caution myself from sharing with a non-running friend over coffee suddenly fall easily out of my mouth when my legs are tired and my heart rate is high.

As we look at this as a way to think about writing, I want to address that word *suffering*. Now, I don't think we need to make ourselves suffer to produce good writing; we don't need to inflict pain upon ourselves, physically or emotionally.

In order to get to "the most authentic version of myself," however, I do need to push myself out of my comfort zone. I need to go places, as a writer, that I've never been before, places that have always been just out of reach, and I have to stretch my intellect and my imagination and my emotions in order to get to those places, and, yes, one of the results is that I'm likely to feel drained or exhausted. (Especially if I'm writing on deadline and I actually *am* pushing myself physically as well—which is not a great strategy, but sometimes it's a necessary one.)

At first, you may have to fight for every insight, every bit of writing that manages to capture what it is you were trying to say. The more time you spend really stretching yourself, though, the more time you spend in those hard-to-reach places, the easier it might become to achieve those insights, to write more and more pages that give you back as much, if not more, than what you've poured into them.

———————

I want to tell you another running story—this one is by Colin Daileda, writing for *Deadspin* about the Hell Ultra, a 298-mile ultramarathon along the Leh-Manali Highway in India. Daileda focused on two men, Pulkit Jain and Shashwat Rao, both of whom wanted to be the first Indian runner to complete the grueling race. I'm not going to tell you what happened because you should track the story down and read it for yourself, but I do want to zero in on this passage at the end:

> Running can obliterate you, because few sports expose people to themselves with such brutality. Its trick is to throw you against the barriers you've built for yourself, then step back innocently to ask what you're going to do about them. Maybe the best way to answer that question is to understand what you want from a run before you begin, and to be prepared to meet something—or someone—out there on the road that can change all that.

Let's think about that in light of the parallel Sakyong Mipham drew between marathon running and writing. I think what Daileda was describing is something that happens to a lot of writers whenever we set out to write something and start to discover what's *really* preoccupying our thoughts and emotions. All those times we tell ourselves, "I'm going to write a story/essay/book about *this*," and then we realize we've been preparing ourselves to grapple with *that* all along. It can be an incredibly frustrating experience, and then suddenly it can become a profoundly liberating one.

I'm not suggesting that the point of a writing practice is to make yourself miserable, or that if you're not miserable, you're doing it wrong. I suppose what I'd say the point was would be to challenge yourself—but that you can challenge yourself without necessarily making yourself miserable because you know, going into that challenge, that it's likely to make you profoundly uncomfortable at some point.

Along those lines, I believe the most useful work for us to be engaged in, and what might prove to be the most interesting work, is the work that tests our writing practice to its limits and forces us to come up with something we didn't realize we were capable of producing *until that moment*. We chase after those moments because we love doing the writing, even when it's hard. Especially when it's hard? Maybe—but, not in a fake-macho masochistic way. ("Look at these pages! They're seasoned *with PAIN!*") That's just empty performance—you won't learn anything meaningful from it, and readers will be able to spot it quickly.

As Carissa Liebowitz says, it's easy to hold things back from other people in our ordinary lives. We're often afraid of burdening people with our stories, or offending them, or driving them away. So we play it safe, show the world an innocuous version of ourselves, one that's not likely to make waves or create awkward moments.

When we sit down to write, we should *live* for making waves. We should live for the awkward . . . well, maybe not all the moments we strive to provoke with our writing are awkward, exactly. Maybe *disruptive* is a better word, one that encompasses not just the awkward, painful stories but the world-changing, upbeat stories as well.

For Liebowitz, running provides a space where she can (forgive the expression) pursue those moments through conversation with others. And, although I'm free-associating a bit here, I guess you could say that every runner has to run their own race, although sometimes they can come together to talk about it afterward—just as every writer has to write their own story, but some of us have the opportunity to connect with other writers and share our stories with people who can understand what we went through to get them.

It can be easy to share our stories with other writers; if we're nervous about the emotional exposure, we can always tell ourselves we're just talking about craft—we're just *analyzing* the story, making sure it *works*. Eventually, though, most of us will need to decide: Am I ready to share this with everyone else?

If you want to focus on things like finding a literary agent or landing a book deal, well, those *are* things you probably should be thinking about at some point if you seriously intend to become a professional writer. But you'll have a better shot at fulfilling those kinds of goals if you can forget the material markers of success for a while and simply keep two questions in mind: "Is this what I want to say? And am I saying it in the clearest way I can right now?"

When you can answer both those questions with a confident, resounding "yes" on a regular basis, you might just find that other good things will start to follow.

Chapter Eight:

Destroy Your Safe and Happy Lives

I n the spring of 2020, just before many of us began sheltering in place in our efforts to flatten the COVID-19 curve—and I remember this distinctly because I made my last trip to the public library to return the book after I was done with it—I read *The Creativity Cure*, a book that was billed as "a do-it-yourself prescription for happiness." The authors, Carrie Barron and Alton Barron, based some of their framework in the psychoanalytic theories of D.W. Winnicott, particularly his notion of the "false self," the persona we create to deal with all the pressures of life, the version of ourselves we show to others to convince them we're exactly as they expect us to be so they won't harm us—as opposed to the "true self," the most authentic, uninhibited expression of our desires. Happiness, in the Barrons' model, comes from acting from your true self as much as possible, and, as they put it, "the *Creative Self* is the happiest, healthiest, and most productive form of the True Self."

The bulk of *The Creativity Cure* concerns itself with how to cultivate that Creative Self—the technique the Barrons outline is an interesting, not not though . . . unexpected, blend of cultivating personal insight and *doing stuff*, the craftier the better. (The dual emphasis makes even more sense when you know Carrie's a psychiatrist and Alton's a hand surgeon.) I don't mean that to be reductive . . . well, okay, I *am* being reductive, but not in a negative way.

Their advice is, as far as I can tell, pretty sound—the sort of commonsense advice many of us just never take the time to actually follow up on because we can't tear ourselves away from all the responsibilities and obligations that fill up our lives and make some *real* changes. Or, sometimes, we half-ass it, and maybe that enables us to feel a little bit better about ourselves, or maybe it doesn't, so we go back to the way things were.

But you're reading *this* book because you want to be one of the people who actually does the work, who creates a sincere expression of your most powerful passions—and then, perhaps, takes the next step of not keeping it to yourself.

If you're interested, you should track down *The Creativity Cure*. It's an easy, perhaps deceptively easy, read. For now, I want to focus on one sentence that stayed with me long after I'd returned the book to the library:

"Process, not product, is what we need to feel alive and well."

When we started sheltering in place, I think a lot of us might actually have been giddy about the prospect of being stuck at home: *We'd get so much work done! We'd have so many words under our belts! And they'd all be great words!*

I don't know how that worked out for you, but I'll be honest: for me, it was a struggle. I was fortunate enough to have some freelance projects, but when I wasn't working on those, there were days I couldn't drag myself out of bed before noon, and evenings where I get caught up in unproductive spirals of rage at the people in every level of government who made things so much worse than they could have been, and that rage drove me to binge games on my smartphone until I looked up and realized it was three in the morning.

Remember that conversation with Dani Shapiro I told you about? At one point, she mentioned that the DNA test results had arrived just after she'd put the finishing touches on her previous memoir, *Hourglass*. If they'd come any earlier, or if work on *Hourglass* had extended much further, she said, "I would have had to put that book aside and probably never would have returned to it . . . It just wasn't where my head was anymore."

If a bestselling author with five novels and five memoirs to her credit can readily admit that her writing practice could be derailed by personal circumstance? Let's take that as a sign of permission that we can cut ourselves a break.

It doesn't have to be as drastic as finding out your father isn't your biological father or a pandemic bringing the entire world to a standstill. If you've hit a rough streak of any kind, and you find yourself struggling to keep up with everything and find yourself not writing, don't beat yourself up over it. Just wait until you can regain control over your time and energy, then figure out how you can reclaim your writing practice. You don't need to make a big deal about it, either; just start up when you have the chance and keep at it as best you can.

A steady writing practice helps us realize what's most important to us, what drives our passions and concerns—and helps us think about reorganizing our lives around those newly discovered priorities. I'd believed that for years, but I *felt* it very keenly in the first few weeks of sheltering in place as all our daily routines were disrupted. My freelance background gave me some experience in working from home, but I imagine the disruption, that feeling of everything coming unmoored many of us felt at the start of the pandemic, might have been especially hard for people who until that moment had been holding down day jobs and finding time for their creative writing when they were at home, whether it was first thing in the morning or last thing at night. If they were lucky enough to have jobs that they could do from home, that could mean the place that had always felt like "my writing space" had been taken over by their professional obligations, making it harder to muster the enthusiasm to switch over to creative writing.

Right around then, advice columnist Heather Havrilesky sent out a newsletter that included this reflection on conquering writer's block:

> It is always better to assume you can write than it is to escape repeatedly into a discussion of how blocked you are or how much you hate writing. Everyone needs to do this *sometimes* but the less you do it . . . the easier it is to write.

I know from personal experience that resisting inertia is easier said than done, but it *can* be done. One thing that worked for me was to create a "buffer space" after finishing a professional assignment, a brief period where I didn't do much more than drink tea and listen to music before moving on to my personal projects. If you work from home and need a similar solution, you might have better luck with yoga—or maybe you're lucky enough to have your own treadmill or exercise bike, or you might be really lucky and have a porch and nice weather so you can create a "creative" space separate from your home workstation.

Or you may have to grit your teeth and write at the same desk or table where you do the work that pays the bills.

For some of us, living through the pandemic *might* result in a more authentic understanding of our lives and what we're meant to be doing, and a batch of new writing that reflects that. But for a lot of us, it won't, and that's okay. I spent a lot of time while we were sheltering in place thinking about *metanoia*, a term from the New Testament that has commonly been translated as "repentance" but might more accurately be called "a change of heart." I've come to recognize that changing your heart isn't so much a finished *result* as an ongoing *process*, and I realized that it's also a useful way to think about pursuing what the Barrons would call our True Self.

You're never going to be perfect. But as long as you're holding *intention* in your heart, and doing your best to act on it, you will inevitably come closer in some way to the things you want to say and the life you want to live. And though you might not be working under optimum conditions, you have as much raw potential to accomplish that as anybody else.

"The weakest among us," wrote the nineteenth-century art critic and social theorist John Ruskin, "has a gift, however seemingly trivial, which is peculiar to him, and which worthily used will be a gift also to his race for ever."

I've long been skeptical about the notion of innate talent, the idea that some people start out with more ability than others, that they're just more "naturally" creative or expressive. As far as I can tell, it's pretty much all skill, and differences in capability come down to how much opportunity a person has been given from an early age to develop that skill, and how much opportunity they've been willing to seize for themselves.

I want to emphasize the role of *how much opportunity a person has been given*. I'm not denying impatience and carelessness and laziness can be traits that get in the way of developing our capability to express ourselves—at the same time, to reiterate a point I've made before: modern society, in all its "Western" capitalist patriarchal glory, is often arranged in ways that withhold creative opportunity from us, and it withholds that opportunity from some of us more deliberately than others. So I don't think that *not* being at the top of your game as a writer represents any kind of moral failing, and I certainly don't think that being at the top of your game as a writer represents any kind of moral success.

Mind you, being at the top of your game as a writer almost always comes with a stronger sense of self-awareness and a stronger recognition of one's personal agenda. A better philosophy scholar than I would be able to tell you whether that, in and of itself, constitutes a "moral success." My instinctive reaction is that the self-awareness we cultivate through a diligent writing practice is not in and of itself a moral success, but that it can be used to achieve one.

———————

The coronavirus pandemic forced many of us into a greater awareness not just of ourselves, but of the pervasive iniquities of the particularly American version of our global capitalist culture and the privileges enjoyed by the White middle and upper classes. We saw this in the way the disease tore through non-White populations that already suffered from diminished access to health care and other public services. Then, in the late spring, three deaths—the killing of Ahmaud Arbery by a retired district attorney's investigator and his two accomplices, the killing of Breonna Taylor during the execution of a "no-knock" warrant by three plainclothes officers, and the killing of George Floyd by a uniformed policeman while three others either helped restrain the victim or prevented anyone from interfering—brought all the anger and frustration of long-simmering issues of race and class to the forefront of American life.

The overlapping public conversations that ensued also included analyses of the biases embedded in our cultural institutions, from public statues honoring the Confederacy to food magazines, and particularly in the literary world. This was not an entirely new discussion, of course; shortly before the pandemic hit, controversy had erupted over *American Dirt*, a thriller written by a White author about a Mexican woman trying to make her way over the border into the United States while being pursued by the drug cartel that had already murdered her husband. Latinx writers were not merely appalled by Jeanine Cummins's representation of their culture and in the way its publisher had promoted the novel, but by the fact that *this* book was rewarded with a million-dollar advance and placement in Oprah's Book Club while works by Latinx authors almost never benefit from such financial windfalls or media largesse.

(Full disclosure: Jeanine is a friend, and someone whose work I've long admired. When I heard she'd gotten a million dollars for a new novel, I was instinctively thrilled for her and for her publishing team, many of whom I also happen to know and like and whom I once, several years ago, sounded out about a job. Corporate publishing and literary culture are, in many ways, small worlds, and that insularity can sometimes be part of the problem.)

Just a few months before *that*, the Romance Writers of America, the preeminent networking and advocacy group within that genre of commercial publishing, collapsed in on itself in spectacular fashion after sanctioning one of its members, Courtney Milan, for violating the organization's ethics guidelines by publicly referring to another writer's novel as a "fucking racist mess." It turned out that, in order to issue that sanction, RWA's leadership had committed several likely ethical violations of its own—largely to massage the wounded ego of the White writer in question and with the added intent of putting Milan, widely recognized for her criticisms of the romance industry's systemic biases, "in her place."

You have to understand that romance fiction is essentially the backbone of commercial book publishing—in and of itself, it brings more than a billion dollars a year into the industry. It's a genre that speaks to a large audience, and to which that large audience eagerly gives its attention. So it matters what gets published. And though romance fiction has made significant strides in recent years, what gets published is still, largely, centered on the interests of heterosexual White women. (There's also a class aspect to be considered, but I'm not capable of doing much more than waving in its general direction.)

Novels written by heterosexual White women for heterosexual White women often did a poor job of representing people of color (or queer people), if they bothered to include representations of such people at all. Milan's criticism, for example, had zeroed in on how a novel from the 1990s, recently republished, relied extensively on stereotypes of Asian women as "demure and quiet." Some writers have been able to push back against this unwanted legacy by creating more positive characters, but much remains to be done in this regard for all marginalized communities.

In part, that's because there's still a profound need for greater diversity and inclusion behind the scenes, where the staff at publishing companies tend to be overwhelmingly White. As long as romance publishers continue to think in terms of, say, "African American readers" or "LGBTQ readers" as niche markets that can be serviced with discrete, finite efforts, they continue to define the mainstream in ways that predominantly cater to heterosexual White women, and writers who can effectively cater to that audience reap the rewards.

Yet so much of what we've seen in the culture at large over the last decade indicates that "the mainstream" is, in fact, becoming much more diverse, or at the very least capable of absorbing much more diversity—that stories with "universal" emotional appeal aren't inherently centered around straight White people.

All of this is to say that there is *plenty* for the literary world to think about with respect to racial inequity. One of the newsletters I've been reading more closely is Kelsey McKinney's *Written Out*, which aims to reconstruct literary history by paying attention to women writers who have been overlooked or underappreciated in the past. In the summer of 2020, McKinney's focus shifted to Black writers, and she reflected on how many magazines, newspapers, and even bookstores were coming up with antiracist reading lists, and how the books on those lists were becoming national bestsellers—which in some respects was great news, but McKinney was justifiably concerned about how such lists, when lazily deployed, "reduce incredible work by black writers to something white people read for self-improvement and not beautiful works on their own."

This, I think, was the heart of her message: "You do not read Nobel Laureate and American Treasure Toni Morrison because you feel bad about being white. You read her because she is arguably the best novelist America has ever produced."

Later, McKinney took what she described as "a hard look at my bookshelf" and realized that despite her best intentions, her reading was still heavily shaped by dominant White culture. I understood her dismay, because I'd gone through a similar self-discovery process eight years ago, grappling with the beam in my own reading eye, particularly concerning gender imbalances. "Book critics, like everybody else, have culturally embedded biases which, when left unchecked, tend to reinforce the status quo," I wrote back then. "In this case, no matter how often prominent figures in the world of literary criticism insist gender plays no role in their decisions about what to review, male writers consistently get the better deal."

Just like McKinney, though, when I sat down and did the math on the book column I was writing at the time, I wasn't much better than the *New York Times* at maintaining a truly diverse personal or professional canon. "Why, despite my intentions, which had already begun to take shape, did I tend to veer toward *this* book rather than *that* one?" I wondered—and what could I do to fix it?

I couldn't fall back on excuses like "these are the books that publishers send me," or more broadly, "these are the books that get published," to justify those results, because that would just be lazy; the books were out there, and it was my job to search for them. I liked to tell myself that I was reviewing books to hold a mirror up to contemporary culture—more often than not to celebrate it, true, but in the broadest sense to engage with it. It seemed, however, that I was at risk of holding a mirror up to myself.

Happily, the literary world seems to be substantially less defensive about its White patriarchal biases than it was back in 2012. It's still *plenty* defensive, mind you; the National Book Critics Circle attempted to craft a statement in solidarity with the Black Lives Matter movement and it ended in a huffy farrago of finger-pointing and mass resignation after the poet and essayist Hope Wabuke publicly circulated an email that had been sent to board members by Philadelphia-based book reviewer Carlin Romano, who resisted this effort by declaring, "I resent the idea that whites in the book publishing and literary world are an oppositional force that needs to be assigned to reeducation camps."

And yet, despite the presence of unreconstructed attitudes like Romano's, people *are* more aware of the problem, and more willing to acknowledge it, than they have been in the past. We don't always know how to fix it, though—and sometimes we're too quick to take the easy way out.

"This isn't the time to circle up with other white people and discuss black pain in the abstract," as Tre Johnson warned in a *Washington Post* op-ed. Reading a few books won't fix the problem, and too many people think that reading the books is all they have to do, especially if they made a big deal of buying those books from a Black-owned independent bookstore.

By all means, read the antiracist books—and, as Kelsey McKinney says, read other books by Black writers "because they are good and we like reading good things." As you read those books, however, make room for them to change your life—*then change your life.*

"The right acknowledgment of black justice, humanity, freedom, and happiness won't be found in your book clubs, protest signs, chalk talks, or organizational statements," Johnson continued. "It will be found in your earnest willingness to dismantle systems that stand in our way—be they at your job, in your social network, your neighborhood associations, your family, or your home."

In *How to Be an Antiracist*, one of the most popular of the books addressing the issue, Ibram X. Kendi tells us there's no such thing as being "non-racist." You're either actively racist, passively complicit in racism, or actively antiracist. It's not that we have an opportunity now to be antiracist—we have *always* had that opportunity, and some of us have failed to seize that opportunity more often than we may care to admit.

That complicity is bound tightly in complacency—and though it may seem strange to talk about complacency considering how many of us have had our lives upended in 2020, I believe it's the right word for the occasion. Fortunately, you don't have to be complacent about systemic racism. We can refuse to accept the status quo and choose a different way of being in this world. Let's acknowledge where we've fallen short and dedicate ourselves to doing better moving forward.

It's not as if we can say that the crises of 2020 caught us unawares—the pandemic, yes, but not the underlying problems permeating our culture, problems that had even wormed their way into the highest levels of government around the world, not just in the United States. In late 2018, for example, the science fiction writer Chuck Wendig was taken off the creative team of a *Star Wars* comic produced by Marvel because "fans" had complained about his behavior on social media. I put "fans" in quotes because it's clear that these people weren't acting out of any enthusiasm for comic books or science fiction, but because they were hatemongers and they considered Wendig to be a "social justice warrior" who had the audacity first, to include a gay character in a *Star Wars* story, and then, to call bigots out on their bigotry when they complained about it.

Marvel apparently decided it was easier to throw Wendig off the back of their sled than it would be to fight off the wolves. "This is really quite chilling," he wrote of how it all went down. "And it breaks my heart. I am very sad, and worried for the country I live in, and the world, and for creative people all around."

In the weeks immediately following, the bigots and, not to put too fine a point on it, the fascists escalated from trying to get people who aren't like them fired to trying to kill those people. And with increasing frequency, they were successful.

It was enough to make you wonder whether it was worth it to keep putting ourselves out there, not just as writers but as human beings. But that's how fascists win—by convincing us that we can't make a difference, that we're powerless to stop them.

Why do we write? I ask myself that all the time, approaching it as a practical question, a philosophical question, a spiritual question, at times an existential question. One of the answers that comes back to me, over and over, is that we write because we have something that we *need* to share with the world, a perspective that we *need* to share with our community . . . and, conversely, that our community needs from us in order to be more complex, more inclusive, more *alive*.

Fascists know that in a world where all stories, all perspectives, are treated with equal consideration, the stories *they* tell about the world aren't compelling enough to attract more than a handful of people. A handful that can be moderately profitable under the right circumstances, but the only way their visions of the world can ever compete against our visions of the world on a widescale basis is for them to manipulate things so they *don't* have to compete with us—by hobbling us or removing us from the playing field entirely.

"I have a dire fear this is going to get a whole lot worse before it gets better," Wendig wrote when he got fired—and, unfortunately, the following two years proved him right.

When Donald Trump was defeated in the presidential election in 2020, it offered many of us a glimmer of hope—but the following two months, which culminated in an insurrectionist mob swarming the United States Capitol in an attempt to derail the certification of that election, proved that the danger is far from behind us. I don't know, of course, where things stand as you read this. Whatever the political state of the world is, though, we need to continue to stand up against hate and tyranny—and, as part of that mission, we need to resist the ongoing effort to silence anyone who offers a perspective that runs counter to the fascist vision.

Part of that comes from resisting external threats of censorship. But we should also resist *internal* threats—the voices in our heads that suggest nothing we say or write will make a difference, or that we're merely distracting ourselves and being selfish when there's *real* work to be done. Sure, political resistance is important. As you used to hear a lot after 9/11, the terrorists win when they force us to change our way of life and live in fear. So, yes, make room for activism in your schedule, but if you have a story to tell, keep trying to make room in your schedule to work at telling it, too. The freedom to tell your own stories, for anyone who's willing to take them in, is a political freedom, too.

Destroy your safe and happy lives before it is too late. Refuse to blindly accept the role the dominant culture does its best to impose upon you—dig relentlessly into your imagination until you find the thing that matters most to you and rebuild your life around paying attention to *that*, nurturing it, and expressing it as clearly and as fully as you can.

While you're at it, make room in your heart for the stories that other people are sharing about what matters most to them. Allow their stories to move you, perhaps even to help you realize something new about your own story—and, just as importantly, work with other writers toward establishing a world that offers everyone the freedom to share their stories you want for yourself.

AS LONG AS YOU'RE HOLDING
INTENTION IN YOUR HEART, AND
DOING YOUR BEST TO ACT ON IT,
YOU WILL INEVITABLY COME
CLOSER IN SOME WAY TO THE
THINGS YOU WANT TO SAY, AND
THE LIFE YOU WANT TO LIVE.

Acknowledgments

First things first: Without the support of my wife, Laura, on myriad levels, you would almost certainly not be reading any of this.

Thanks to Anne Trubek at Belt Publishing for her receptivity and enthusiasm when I wrote to her asking if a collection of essays from my newsletter might be of interest, and to my editor, Dan Crissman, who helped shape the various fragments into a coherent whole. Any errors in the resulting text are my own responsibility. And thanks, too, to Martha Bayne for her work in helping this book find its audience.

I reached out to the artist Emm Roy with the idea that she might be able to provide some original illustrations. While she was reviewing the manuscript to make sure she'd be comfortable taking that on, she ended up identifying more than a few spots where I hadn't thought through my language as thoroughly as I could have, and her suggestions have, I hope, made this a more welcoming and inclusive book. *AND* her drawings are fantastic! I encourage everyone to look for Emm on Instagram (@emmnotemma) or support her through Patreon.

If what you've read here has inspired you, and you'd like to read more like it on a regular basis, *Destroy Your Safe and Happy Lives* is online at ronhogan.substack.com and updated regularly. From there, you can sign up to have it emailed to you for free.

Resources (An Incomplete Reckoning)

Chapter One: What We Carry in Our Hearts
"The Profession of Author in the 21st Century" is available at the Authors Guild website and offers a sobering look at the economic realities of the literary world. The Thomas Merton quote comes from his essay "Learning to Live." The Henri Nouwen quote originally comes from his book *Spiritual Direction*. The details of Lutgardis's visions of Jesus come from her contemporary biographer, Thomas of Cantimpré.

Chapter Two: An Adventure into an Unknown World
I love Lawrence Weschler's *Mr. Wilson's Cabinet of Wonder*, along with all his other books. Jim Bouton's *Ball Four* is usually packaged these days with its sequel, *Ball Five*. The PBS documentary about Mark Rothko is *Rothko: Pictures Must Be Miraculous*. The letter from Rothko and Adolph Gottlieb to the art editor at the *New York Times* is online in a few different places. I saw *The Lost Bird Project* one night on PBS; keep an eye out for it!

Chapter Three: Our Endless and Proper Work
Conan O'Brien spoke to Dave Itzkoff in early 2019 for a *New York Times* feature, "Conan O'Brien Wants to Scare Himself With the New, Shorter 'Conan.'" A good place to start with Mary Oliver is her selected poems in *Devotions*. Hannah Gadsby's *Nanette* should still be on Netflix, if they're smart. Jeffrey Kripal's books are as captivating as

they are intellectually rigorous. I'm pretty sure the Geoffrey Owens interview I'm thinking of was on the *Today* show and should still be on YouTube.

Chapter Four: Reclaiming Your Time for Writing

I'm not sure where I first read about Dunbar's number, but the most likely candidate is Malcolm Gladwell's *The Tipping Point*. Amanda Petrusich's "Going Home with Wendell Berry" appeared in the *New Yorker* in the summer of 2019. John Eldredge's *Restoration Year* is another of the books from my devotional practice; he's a bit more conservatively evangelical than I tend to go for, but there's a lot of useful insights in there. Bryan Edward Hill's *Black Lightning/Hong Kong Phooey* should be available at your local comic book shop.

Chapter Five: Finding Your Groove

James Clear's *Atomic Habits* is very easy to find. Farrah Penn wrote "This Woman Wrote Her Novel at a Tire Store and Now They Are Her Biggest Fans" for Buzzfeed in 2018. Lindsay Ellis recently published her first novel, *Axiom's End*.

Chapter Six: Your Voice Is Valuable

In addition to *Things I Don't Want to Know* and *The Cost of Living*, you should read Deborah Levy's fiction. My interview with Dani Shapiro appeared in the *Dallas Morning News* in early 2019. Seanan McGuire has written many excellent novels under her own name and as Mira Grant. Heather Demetrios published "How to Lose a Third of a Million Dollars Without Really Trying" on Medium in

2018. In addition to *Creativity, Spirituality, and Making a Buck*, David Nichtern also wrote *Awakening from the Daydream*, which I found even more useful in ways I might be able to write about one day.

Chapter Seven: Pacing Yourself for the Long Haul
Sakyong Mipham's *Running with the Mind of Meditation* should be pretty easy to track down. T*he Half Marathoner* is an excellent newsletter you can find online at Substack, the same platform I use for *Destroy Your Safe and Happy Lives*. Colin Dailed's "To Win An Ultramarathon Through Hell, You Need A Devil To Chase" was published at *Deadspin* in 2019.

Chapter Eight: Destroy Your Safe and Happy Lives
If your local bookstore or public library doesn't have *The Creativity Cure*, they should be able to get it in upon request. Heather Havrilesky has *two* great Substack newsletters you'll want to read: *Ask Molly* and *Ask Polly*. I'm not sure where I found that Ruskin quote, to be honest. Kelsey McKinney's newsletter is available on Substack, too. (Her debut novel, *God Spare the Girls*, is coming out around the same time as this book.) Tre Johnson's "When Black People Are in Pain, White People Just Join Book Clubs" appeared in the *Washington Post* in June 2020. I can't recommend Ibram X. Kendi's *How to Be an Antiracist* highly enough. Chuck Wendig shared his concerns on Twitter; he has a whole bunch of novels you should read.

CPSIA information can be obtained
at www.ICGtesting.com
Printed in the USA
JSHW022058160521
14732JS00005B/7